TRUSTING YOU
THE JOURNEY TO UNAPOLOGETICALLY LEARNING TO LISTEN, BELIEVE, AND TRUST YOURSELF AGAIN

CHRISTY TRUJILLO

burning soul press

CONTENTS

DISCLAIMER

This book is a reflection of my personal journey through pain, healing, and rediscovery. It represents my thoughts, emotions, and interpretations of events as I experienced them. The purpose of sharing these reflections is not to assign blame, expose others, or relive past wounds, but to offer hope to those who are navigating their own seasons of hardship and transformation.

While parts of this book reference pivotal moments from my past relationships, marriages, and life events, I have intentionally chosen to share my *perspective* rather than recount the actions or identities of others involved. Out of respect for privacy and in accordance with existing agreements, identifying details have been omitted or altered when necessary.

Nothing in this book is intended to be disparaging or defamatory. My intention is solely to speak to the emotional landscape of healing, not to cast judgment or invite speculation.

If you are walking through your own loss, betrayal, or uncertainty, my hope is that this story reminds you that you are not alone—and that healing is not only possible, but powerful.

For the woman who's held her breath through the longest nights, carried the weight of worry for her children, and whispered prayers into the dark.

Every hardship holds a lesson, every scar a quiet wisdom.

You are stronger than you know, braver than you feel, and never as alone as you think.

You will trust yourself again— and when you do, you'll see that she was within you all along.

INTRODUCTION: TRUSTING YOURSELF AGAIN

At 50 years old, I was supposed to be settling into predictable routines, not getting my first tattoo. Growing up as the daughter of a country doctor and a Cuban immigrant in Texas, tattoos weren't exactly part of the plan. But there I was, having the words "Fear not, for I am with you" - Isaiah 41:10 - etched down my spine. Those words had become my lifeline, my foundation when trust seemed impossible— through cancer treatments, a devastating business lawsuit, and the end of my twenty-three-year marriage when every pillar I had built my life upon was crumbling simultaneously.

Trust had been broken in every direction. Yet somehow, I found myself trusting again—not because it was easy, but because it was necessary. Sometimes the very thing that shatters your trust becomes the catalyst for building something stronger than before.

Trust isn't just broken in dramatic moments—though Lord knows I've had my share of those. More often, it erodes gradually, like water wearing away stone. A dismissive comment here. A gut feeling ignored there. A small compromise that leads to bigger ones. Before you know it, you're standing in the ruins of what was once solid ground, wondering how in the world everything collapsed.

I remember sitting in my kitchen during my divorce mediation, gripping the counter as I mindlessly stirred brownie batter. What was supposed to be a four-hour Zoom mediation had stretched into nine grueling hours. My sister had come to sit with me after sensing I shouldn't be alone, and as we waited between attorney discussions, I baked— my stress response taking over. During one of those long pauses, the reality of it all hit me. "How did I get here?" I whispered, tears streaming down my face as my sister quietly watched. "How did I miss so many signs?" The pandemic had forced this life-altering process onto a screen, making it somehow both more distant and more intimate as my marriage officially unraveled in the same space where we'd once built a life together.

But when you discover violations of your trust that span years, you don't just lose your future—you lose your past. Every memory gets reexamined through a different lens. Had those happy moments I remembered actually been happy, or had I been blind to what was really happening? Were the milestones we celebrated together—anniversaries, birthdays, family vacations—genuine, or was I living in a carefully constructed facade?

It's a special kind of grief, mourning not just what you've lost, but questioning whether what you thought you had was ever real in the first place. That romantic dinner where he seemed distracted—where was his mind at? That time he was working late—was he really working? All those nights I went to bed without him, why was he not there with me? Those moments when my intuition whispered something was wrong—why didn't I trust it?

Cancer had threatened my body, but divorce threatened something deeper—my ability to trust my own perceptions, my own memories, my own reality. And that kind of uncertainty cuts deeper than any physical pain I've ever experienced.

The truth is, I hadn't missed the signs. I had seen them, felt them, known them deep in my bones—but I had talked myself out of trusting what I knew. I had become so accustomed to doubting my perceptions that ignoring my intuition had become second nature.

Perhaps you know this feeling too. Maybe it wasn't a health crisis or the end of a long marriage, but you've experienced that moment when you realized you'd been betraying yourself by not honoring what you knew to be true. Maybe you stayed in a toxic friendship because you didn't trust that you deserved better. Maybe you remained in a soul-crushing job because you didn't believe in your own capabilities. Maybe you silenced yourself in an important conversation because you doubted the value of your voice.

That's the insidious nature of broken self-trust—it doesn't just affect one decision; it infiltrates every area of your life. When I finally understood this, I realized that rebuilding trust with myself wasn't optional—it was fundamental to everything else I wanted to create in my life. Without it, I would keep repeating patterns that led me right back to brokenness.

It took having my whole world turned upside down to realize that even when everything else is stripped away, I was still there. The real me. The one who'd been there all along, waiting to be honored, to be rediscovered, to be trusted—and that's what I want to help you find in yourself too.

This book is about the journey we all face at some point —that journey back to ourselves. Whether you're dealing with betrayal, facing down a scary diagnosis, trying to figure out what's next in your career, or feeling lost in your own life, I want you to know something: you can rebuild. Not just survive, but actually thrive as your true authentic self.

I think of trust like a tree. The roots—your core ability to know yourself, where you came from, and what you need— are always there, even when you can't see them. Sometimes the visible parts look damaged or withered because we haven't nourished our self-trust properly. We might even feel completely disconnected from our ability to trust our own judgment. But those roots are still intact beneath the surface, waiting for the right conditions to help us flourish again.

Trusting yourself isn't always easy. Lord knows I've spent more nights than I can count second-guessing my decisions, wondering if I was strong enough to handle what was in front of me. But that's exactly when trust matters most—when the path isn't clear, when your knees are shaking, when your heart is unsure.

The path to trusting yourself again is more like a spiral than a straight line—we keep circling back to the same lessons, just at deeper levels each time. That's how we finally get it into our bones. In this book, I'm breaking the journey into four parts that build on each other.

The **Foundations of Self-Trust** is exploring how our roots, resilience, and even our quirks (yes, those things that make you different!) create the bedrock of who you are. I've learned that the very things that made me feel awkward or "too much" have become my superpowers, and I bet the same is true for you.

When Trust is Broken is how we lose faith in ourselves through tough choices, betrayal, and those storms that come out of nowhere. We all have our stories of broken trust, and understanding what happens in our hearts and minds when trust shatters is super important for healing.

Then comes the good part—**Rebuilding Trust**. This is where we learn to sort out which voice is really yours among all the noise, discover your internal "peace meter" (that gut feeling that tells you when something's off), and rewire those pathways in your brain that keep you stuck in doubt.

Finally, we'll explore what it means to **Live in Trust**— starting over after your world falls apart, taking those scary next steps when you can't see the whole path, and embracing this crazy journey as something worth trusting.

Through my own roller-coaster journey and working with hundreds of women, I've noticed that self-trust stands on four pillars that we'll also explore throughout this book.

Trusting Your Perception: This is about believing what you see, feel, and experience without needing someone else to validate it. It's that moment when you think, "I'm not crazy —this really is happening," and you stand in that truth even when others don't see it.

Trusting Your Decisions: This is developing confidence in your ability to make choices that align with who you really are, even when they disappoint people you love. It's saying, "This is right for me" and actually believing it.

Trusting Your Resilience: This is believing in your capacity to handle whatever comes your way—even the stuff that feels impossible. It's knowing that even if things go sideways, you'll figure it out.

Trusting Your Wisdom: This is recognizing that your life experiences—even the messy ones—have given you valuable insights that deserve respect, especially from yourself! It's about honoring the wisdom you've earned the hard way.

When these pillars are strong, you move through life with this quiet confidence that doesn't depend on everything going perfectly. You know you'll handle whatever comes. You don't need everyone to agree with your choices because you're anchored in what you know to be true for you. And let me tell you, that kind of freedom changes everything.

Self-trust isn't just some fluffy concept—it's literally wired into our brains! Our minds create patterns based on our experiences. When we keep overriding our gut feelings or let someone convince us we're wrong about what we know to be true, we're actually creating neural pathways that make us doubt our automatic response.

The science folks call this neuroplasticity—our brains physically change based on our thought patterns. When you constantly doubt yourself, your brain gets super efficient at generating more doubt. It's like your brain thinks, "Oh, she doubts herself all the time, so I'll just keep those doubt pathways nice and strong!"

But here's the amazing part that gave me so much hope during my darkest days: we can create new pathways. We can literally rewire our brains toward trust through consistent, intentional practices. I wasn't permanently broken—I was just operating from old wiring that no longer served me. And with some dedicated effort and the right support, I could create new pathways. And so can you!

What makes this journey different from other approaches to rebuilding trust? I'm not going to give you a list of steps to follow or promise you'll be "fixed" in 30 days. Instead, I'm going to show you how to recognize the whispers of your own inner wisdom that have been there all along. This isn't about becoming someone new—it's about remembering who you've always been beneath the layers of doubt and second-guessing. And it's about understanding that your faith and your intuition aren't separate things—they're partners in guiding you home to yourself.

I'm sharing my story throughout this book not because it's anything special, but because I know you'll see pieces of yourself in it. Most importantly, I'll give you practical tools that have helped me and hundreds of women I've coached through their own rebuilding journeys.

But there's the thing, this isn't the kind of book you want to race through. Trust me on this one! Each chapter is designed to help you dig into your own relationship with trust, so I'd really recommend keeping a journal as you read. Jot down what hits you, what makes you go "hmm," and where you start seeing patterns in your own life.

You'll probably notice that some chapters really get to you while others might not hit as hard—that's exactly how it should be! We all have different places where our trust got dinged up, different pillars that need some extra support. Listen to your gut about what you need right now, because trust isn't something I can hand you—it's something you've got to reclaim for yourself.

My faith is woven all through my story because it's been

my lifeline. But even if you don't share my exact beliefs, the journey of reconnecting with your inner wisdom is pretty universal. We're all just trying to find our way back to ourselves, right?

One scripture that has become my absolute anchor is Proverbs 3:5 (NIV): "Trust in the Lord with all your heart, and lean not on your own understanding." Trusting yourself doesn't mean you always know the answer or have perfect judgment; it means believing in your ability to listen to God's guidance, to figure things out step by step, to grow through the hard times. It's about recognizing when He's opening a door and when He's closing one. It means understanding that your foundation is still there, even when the storms of life have left you feeling broken and exposed. Your roots run deeper than you know, and true self-trust is actually grounded in something greater than yourself.

This is the freedom I want for you—the freedom that comes from truly trusting yourself again. Not because you've never been wrong (we've all messed up!), but because you know your worth isn't determined by your mistakes. Not because you'll never face betrayal again, but because you know you can survive it if you do.

And no matter how many times life knocks you down, you have everything you need inside you to stand back up, dust yourself off, and say: "I'm still here. I'm still me. And I'm ready for what comes next."

As you read these pages, I invite you to see your own story reflected in mine. Where have you lost trust in yourself? What would be possible if you reclaimed it? This journey back to ourselves isn't just about healing—it's about becoming more fully who we were always meant to be.

PART ONE
FOUNDATIONS OF SELF-TRUST

CHAPTER ONE

TRUSTING YOUR ROOTS

THE NAME OF THE STREET WHERE I FOUND MY NEW BEGINNING couldn't have been more perfect: Liberty Lane.

As I hung pictures on the walls of my new home—creating a sanctuary that reflected who I truly was for perhaps the first time in my life—I felt something unexpected bloom inside me: recognition. Not because everything was perfect. Far from it. I was starting over at forty-eight, rebuilding a life for myself and my daughters after my 23-year marriage had ended. By most measures, I should have been terrified.

But in this place where I could finally be fully myself, I wasn't becoming someone new. I was reconnecting with who I'd always been. Hope, I discovered, doesn't always come from what lies ahead. Sometimes it comes from what has always been inside you, waiting to be trusted again.

More than just surviving, I was reclaiming something essential that had been buried under years of doubt and compromise. I was remembering who I had always been beneath the roles and expectations. And in that remembering came the realization that the very roots I had sometimes resented—the farm work, the discipline, the feeling of being different—had been silently preparing me for this moment all along.

These roots I was rediscovering? They'd been planted decades earlier with words that echoed through my childhood: "Idle hands are the devil's workshop." Whether I was filing patient records in my father's medical practice, mending fences on our 650-acre farm, or helping my mother harvest heirloom tomatoes. The phrase wasn't just a saying in our house—it was a foundation, as deeply rooted as the Cuban values my mother brought with her when she fled Castro's regime at fifteen, and as firmly planted as my father's reputation as a "country doctor" in the Dallas area.

I grew up straddling worlds that, on the surface, seemed to have nothing in common. There was the farm girl who drove around with my dad checking on cattle—one of the "gate girls" as he called me and my two sisters, always ready to hop out and open the next fence—and the city girl who collected Italian Vogue magazines and dreamed of catwalks. My father's medical practice taught me precision; the farm taught me perseverance; my mother's immigrant story taught me resilience.

At the time, I thought these contradictions made me strange, out of place. I'd find myself sitting in school, mud still caked under my fingernails from the weekend at the farm, irritated that I had missed the after-game hangouts because we had to leave right after I finished cheering at the Friday night football game. I'd flip through fashion magazines while other girls talked about normal weekend plans, feeling like I didn't fully belong in either world. I wondered if God had somehow mixed up my wiring. Why couldn't I just fit neatly into one world like everyone else seemed to?

What I couldn't see then was that I was learning not to trust my own complexity. I was teaching myself that being multi-faceted was a problem to solve rather than a strength to embrace. Every time I felt torn between these different parts of myself, I was unconsciously deciding that my perceptions of who I was couldn't be trusted.

What I couldn't possibly understand until much later was how God was using these very contradictions to prepare me for every challenge that would come. He wasn't confused about who I was meant to be. He was creating a tapestry with threads I couldn't yet see the purpose for.

My dad, born and raised in Dallas, came from a family of entrepreneurs. His father owned a chain of hamburger stands called Here'tis—not just as a business owner, but as a hands-on worker. My grandparents were there day in and day out, flipping burgers and baking pies. Keeping a restaurant running successfully was sweat-of-your-brow kind of work. It seeped into every pore of my father's being.

Daddy took that work ethic and channeled it into becoming the first in his family to earn a degree and become a physician. To him, medicine wasn't just a career; it was a calling, a way to serve his community. He'd see patients all day in his practice, then make rounds at three different hospitals, and still find time to work our 650-acre farm, tending to the animals and half acre garden with as much dedication as he did his patients.

He had high expectations of success, achievement, and a job well done for himself and for all of those around him, and it was drilled into us at an early age.

From age twelve, my two sisters and I worked in his

medical practice. We'd be filing papers, answering phones, and learning the rhythm of a busy clinic. Then weekends would find us at the farm, our self manicured clinic nails now caked with dirt as we pulled weeds, pruned fruit trees, and harvested whatever was in season.

As tough as my dad was (and boy, was he tough), there was a softer side to him too that would appear on rare occasions. Every morning, he had a ritual. He'd sit in bed, and my mom would bring him his coffee and newspaper. We girls would take turns sitting on his lap while he read. It might have only been for two or three minutes, but those moments of connection were priceless.

My family's idea of quality time was sweating it out together on our farm. I'd love to tell you I embraced this with enthusiasm, but let's be real. Building fences and planting onion slips isn't exactly a teenage girl's idea of a good time. There were many times I longed for a "normal" childhood.

We would joke in my family that Daddy would "make work" if we were sitting down. He'd always create something for us to do because "there was always something to do." My mom would do the same if we had friends over. She would find things for us to help with. My friends still joke about it. Take our annual corn harvest around the 4th of July. While watching fireworks, we were outside with our friends, shucking what felt like a million ears of corn. We'd set up these massive pots of boiling water by the grill, blanching corn like our lives depended on it.

It was hot, sticky work, but there was something magical about it too. The laughter, the shared sense of accomplishment, the sweet taste of that fresh corn—I may have been missing out on weekend pool parties with my friends, but later on in life, it gave me an appreciation for how good productivity can actually feel when it's put toward something meaningful.

As much as I complained, those experiences shaped me in ways I never expected. I was learning to find meaning in hard work—not just any work, but work that connected me to something bigger than myself.

Looking back, I realize that all those long hours working alongside my sisters forged a bond between us that nothing could break. While our father's strict discipline sometimes felt overwhelming, we leaned on each other, finding strength in our shared experiences. Through every challenge, my sisters became my confidantes and closest allies. Today, they remain my best friends and have been for decades—a sisterhood strengthened by sweat equity and shared resilience that has become fundamental to who I am.

Sometimes the people who've weathered the same storms with you become the most reliable voices in your life. When you're questioning your own perceptions later, these are the people who remember your strength when you've forgotten it.

When I was twelve, I was riding horses with my sisters. My older sister was on one horse, and my younger sister and I were on another. As we rounded a big cedar tree, our horse lost sight of my sister's, panicked, and took off at full speed. Then, just as suddenly, it stopped. My younger sister and I went flying off its back, crashing hard into the dirt.

My older sister galloped back to our little cabin to get my dad. By the time he arrived, we were sobbing on the ground. But instead of offering comfort, he made us get back on the horse. I climbed back on with knees shaking, certain I'd get thrown again.

I remember the terror going through my body. My hands shook so badly I could barely hold the reins. Every ounce of me wanted to run away, not climb back on the very animal that had just thrown me to the ground. My heart pounded so hard I could feel it in my ears, drowning out everything except my own panic. Cold sweat beaded on my forehead despite the Texas heat. My breath came in short, shallow gasps that made me lightheaded. I felt angry, humiliated, and completely misunderstood.

"Daddy, please," I begged, tears streaming down my face. "I can't."

But his expression didn't soften. "You can and you will," he said.

At that moment, I had a choice: trust my father's belief in me or trust my fear. The shaking in my hands was real. The terror was real. But so was the quiet voice that said, "You can do this."

Each step toward the house was a small victory over fear. By the time we reached the front of the pasture, something had shifted inside me. The fear was still there, but something else had taken root alongside it—a quiet knowing that I could face what terrified me and survive.

All of these experiences in my upbringing, the good and the bad, became my compass, guiding me through life's ups and downs. When faced with challenges in my career or personal life, I could always draw on that stubborn determination I learned on the farm to get back up on the horse no matter what. I realized those moments were teaching me something invaluable that would play in key times in my future—how to create my own opportunities through perseverance and never give up.

WHEN ROOTS BECOME LIFELINES

In fifth grade, I did a tree project where I identified all the different leaves we have on the farm. I loved it because to this day, I think about trees a lot.

One of my favorite facts is that the ones with the strongest trunks have the deepest, most complex root systems. Those roots aren't always pretty—they're gnarled, they twist around obstacles, they go deep when they need to and spread wide other times. But every weird bend and unusual growth serves a purpose.

In life, the roots that sometimes felt most restricting were often the ones that provided the most support when life's storms came. Just like a tree that's weathered wind and drought develops stronger, more complex roots, our most challenging experiences often build the foundation for our greatest resilience.

There's something powerful about trusting your roots, even the ones that might seem twisted or imperfect. For years, I tried to minimize certain aspects of my upbringing. I downplayed my interest in fashion because it seemed frivolous compared to the serious work ethic I was raised with. I minimized my farm background in certain professional settings where it didn't seem "sophisticated" enough.

But what I've learned is that there's incredible strength in embracing the full complexity of where you come from. Every part of my background contributed to who I am. My father's unyielding standards taught me to push through when things got hard. My mother's immigrant experience taught me that you can start over and thrive in new circumstances. When I've had to reinvent my career, I found myself channeling my parents' entrepreneurial spirits. The farm taught me that consistent effort yields results, even when the work isn't glamorous.

Learning to trust your roots doesn't mean you have to love every aspect of your upbringing. Lord knows there were times when I resented the never-ending work, the lack of free time with friends, the constant pressure to achieve. I resented the extreme rules we had, such as "Do not talk to boys" and "You don't date until you're 16."

But trusting your roots means recognizing how even the difficult parts have shaped you in important ways. Your roots aren't just where you come from—they're where you find your strength when everything else is stripped away.

Decades later, when I sat in the cold, sterile room hearing a cancer diagnosis, that same paralyzing fear from riding the horse gripped me. My hands trembled just as they had on that horse. The world narrowed to a terrifying point, and every instinct screamed to run away. But this time, the voice that steadied me wasn't my father's—it was deeper, calmer. "Do not fear. You have this," I heard within my spirit. It was the Lord's voice guiding me. As I had learned on that horse years ago, I didn't need to flee the fear—I needed to ride through it.

During those grueling months of treatment, my body weakened but my resolve strengthened. The discipline of showing up day after day for radiation, of pushing through bone-deep fatigue to care for my young daughters, of maintaining my business when I could barely stand—all of it drew from that well of persistence dug during those long farm days. As an entrepreneur, if I didn't work, I didn't get paid, so I had to keep pushing forward no matter how I felt. When other patients marveled at my ability to maintain a positive outlook, I recognized it wasn't some inherent quality. It was a muscle built through years of doing what needed to be done, regardless of how I felt about it.

Right on the cusp of my marriage crumbling, a devastating lawsuit from my former company attacked not only my livelihood but also the integrity and reputation I had worked relentlessly to build. Yet even in the face of this dual crisis, that same resilience carried me through. There were days when getting out of bed felt as impossible as climbing back on that horse. But that's the thing about roots—they hold you steady even when you can't see them. The discipline of showing up, of doing the hard thing, of persisting when every fiber of your being wants to quit—these were life lessons that became my salvation when everything else fell apart.

FINDING YOUR EDGE IN YOUR ROOTS

One thing I can say for certain is that God doesn't waste anything—not even the pain, not even the parts that don't seem to fit together. I now see that straddling different worlds wasn't my weakness but my superpower. It wasn't an accident that I could speak the language of cardiologists and farmers. It wasn't a mistake that I understood both high fashion and hard labor. Because of those experiences, I can relate easily to a wide range of people, which not only lights my heart on fire, but has served me well in my professional life. We think it's so easy to "get off track" when really, every single step we take is preparing us for something important down the road. The key is having trust in what was as well as trust in what will be. Nothing in your journey is wasted if you're willing to learn from it.

This is the hidden power of our complicated roots—they're not just where we come from, they're precisely what gives us our unique edge in this world.

I spent decades trying to fit into other people's molds—trying to be more like my sister since I look up to her, my colleagues, even what I thought a "proper Christian woman" should be. But through tear-soaked prayers and quiet revelation I realized that God doesn't create carbon copies. He creates originals, and your originality is found precisely in those places where your story seems messy or contradictory. My daughter taught me this more than anyone in the most beautiful way (I'll share more later)—watching her embrace her unique qualities showed me how God intentionally makes us different to bring our individual strengths to the world.

You aren't born to fit in a box of someone else's definition! You're meant to break free from those constraints and embrace the unique, beautiful person God created you to be—with all your complexities, strengths, and unexpected gifts.

So, let me ask you: do you know what your unique edge is and how your roots give life to it?

If not (or even if you do know), think about your life, and take a moment to reflect:

• What parts of your background have you been trying to minimize that might actually be your greatest strength?

• How have your past experiences of feeling different prepared you for where you are now?

• What contradictions in your life might actually be creating your unique edge?

• Where are you still trying to fit into someone else's mold instead of trusting your unique combination of experiences?

• What problem do you solve in a way that surprises others because of your unique perspective?

Your edge isn't about having everything figured out. I sure didn't! It's about standing in the middle of your contradictions and saying, "Yes, all of this is me."

Trusting your roots means honoring your unique story. It's about embracing the experiences that shaped you, even the difficult ones, as vital preparation for where you're going. On a practical level, it means making decisions that align with your core values, pursuing passions that light you up inside (even if they seem impractical), and treating your inner voice as your most trusted guide.

Your roots aren't just your history—they're your foundation. Every contradiction, every struggle, every moment that made you feel different has been quietly preparing you for something you can't see yet.

Your roots have given you a unique way of seeing the world, and learning to trust that perception—even when others can't see what you see—is where self-trust begins. Because if you can't trust your own eyes, your own experiences, your own knowing, how can you trust anything else?

The question isn't whether your roots are perfect. The question is whether you're brave enough to trust them as the foundation for everything you're meant to become.

Your roots aren't holding you back—they're holding you up.

CHAPTER TWO

TRUSTING YOUR RESILIENCE

THE GREATEST MISCONCEPTION ABOUT RESILIENCE IS THAT IT'S about being unbreakable. It's not. True resilience is about trusting that when you do break, you can rebuild yourself into something even stronger. But man, that's so hard to do in the thick of it.

I've learned that resilience and trust are two sides of the same coin. You cannot build one without the other.

When life delivers its inevitable blows, resilience doesn't ask if you're strong enough to withstand them. It asks if you trust yourself enough to be transformed by them.

My understanding of this began long before I experienced my own trials. In fact, resilience was sewn into the very fabric of my family history, quite literally.

When Fidel Castro took over Cuba, my mother's family found themselves at a crossroads. As Castro began requiring children to work in sugarcane fields for six weeks, returning home only on weekends, my grandmother drew her line in the sand. She declared it was time for them to leave. But leaving wasn't as simple as booking a flight. They had to be secretive, strategic, and above all, brave.

My great-grandfather, understanding they would need resources to rebuild their lives, took my fifteen-year-old mother to buy three pieces of fine jewelry. She picked them out herself, with the understanding that if they needed to sell them, she would have to be okay with it. The pieces were innocent enough for a young girl traveling, but valuable enough to provide a financial safety net if needed.

More ingeniously, he had American checks from the family's grocery store business carefully sewn into the hem of my mother's skirt. Those hidden checks represented more than money; they embodied hope, possibility, and the foresight of a man who understood that sometimes survival requires both preparation and audacity.

They left everything else behind—their home, their possessions, their entire way of life. Yet what they carried with them was far more valuable: resilience, determination, and an unwavering trust that they could rebuild.

Unlike most Cuban immigrants who found community in Miami's welcoming shores, my mother's family landed in Dallas, Texas in 1960, where Spanish was as rare as palm trees. She was the only Spanish-speaking student in her entire high school, a reality that seems almost unimaginable in today's Dallas, where the halls of that same school now echo with more Spanish than English.

In Dallas, a local church, White Rock United Methodist Church, helped them find housing, which was just the beginning of their challenges. My grandfather was sick and unable to work full-time. My uncle was mentally handicapped, requiring constant care and attention. And my mother, at fifteen, found herself navigating not just a new country, but a new language, new customs, and a level of responsibility that would have crushed many adults, let alone a teenager.

When I asked my mother if she ever felt secondary to her brother's needs, if she ever felt neglected amid all the family's challenges, her response was immediate and firm: "No, I still got all the love I needed."

I've come to believe that resilience is often born in seasons of scarcity. For my family, every penny was saved. Every resource was carefully managed. My grandmother would save ketchup packets from Whataburger to use at home. Some might view this as extreme frugality, but I see it differently now. It wasn't about being cheap—it was about respecting resources, understanding their true value, and never taking anything for granted.

When my younger sister was planning her wedding, and we were touring lavish venues in Dallas, my mother broke down in tears—something I rarely witnessed. "I just can't stomach spending this kind of money even though we could," she said. "There are people who don't have things they need. This is not necessary." She wasn't denying us nice things. She was helping us understand the difference between what you can do and what you should do.

Despite these challenges in her upbringing—or perhaps because of them—my mother thrived. She earned a full scholarship to Southern Methodist University, borrowing the family car to drive herself to classes.

My grandmother refused to let circumstances define their possibilities. Education was key in my mom's family, and it became even more sacred after they lost everything in Cuba. My mom used to say, "Someone can take away your money, but they can't take your knowledge and education."

This philosophy became the foundation of their new life in America.

This resilience, this ability to trust in the process of rebuilding, became the backbone of how she raised us. Where others might have seen hardship, she saw character building. Where others might have gotten lost in self-pity, she found purpose. Even now, in my own moments of challenge, I hear her voice clearly: "Put this in perspective."

More than family legends, these stories became my roadmap for resilience. Every time I face adversity, I've heard those same voices of generations of resilient women speaking through me, reminding me that our circumstances don't define us, our response to them does.

Life has taught me to make a practice of approaching challenges with purpose rather than fear. When faced with difficult situations, I often create rituals that transform what could be periods of despair into opportunities for unexpected growth. Some may want to call it toxic positivity when it's actually a strategic resilience, a deliberate choice to find meaning even in suffering.

One practice I've found particularly powerful is rather than pushing through difficult days, I intentionally look for where God is reminding me of blessings throughout the day. When I'm struggling, I slow down and open my eyes to the gifts that might otherwise go unnoticed in the rush. Recently, during a particularly difficult day, instead of hurrying through my to-do list, I felt prompted to stop by a friend's home. What started as dropping something off turned into an invitation for coffee and meaningful conversations with people I wouldn't have otherwise met if I didn't slow down that day.

These moments of grace appear in countless ways—a

sweet text from one of my daughters, a thoughtful message from a team member, an unexpected moment of beauty on my drive. Rather than being so busy that I miss them, I've learned to proactively seek out these small blessings. It's not about distracting myself from problems, but about shifting my perspective to recognize God's presence even in difficult seasons. This practice doesn't eliminate struggles, but it does change how I move through them, helping me maintain gratitude regardless of what challenges I'm facing. Like my mother's philosophy, even in hardship, we can choose our perspective.

YOUR RESILIENCE INVENTORY

When life presents us with trials—and it will—we have a choice. We can resist them, fight them, wish them away. Or we can trust them as teachers, accept them as guides, welcome them as opportunities to add another layer to our family's legacy of resilience.

I've learned to collect evidence of my resilience in practical ways. Years ago, I created what I called my "Glory File"—a literal file folder before everything went digital. Inside were notes I'd received with compliments or words of encouragement, little reminders of my worth I could turn to when I wasn't feeling good about myself. It was my tangible proof that I was capable, loved, and stronger than I sometimes believed.

This inventory of resilience takes many forms. When I went for a scan during my breast cancer treatment, I deliberately wore my mother's diamond set in my grandmother's worn wedding band. I had stopped wearing it regularly after my first daughter was born because the band had gotten so thin, but on that day, I needed that physical reminder that strong women came before me, women who had faced incredibly difficult challenges and emerged with great strength. Those rings connected me to my lineage of resilience.

Think about a time when you felt completely broken by circumstances. Maybe it was a job loss, a health crisis, a relationship ending, or a dream dying. At that moment, trust probably felt impossible. Yet somehow, you rebuilt. You expanded beyond what you thought were your limits. You transformed.

That transformation wasn't accidental—it was inevitable once you trusted the process enough to stay in it. Once you stopped asking "Why me?" and started asking "What for?" Once you recognized that growth often requires breaking old boundaries and comfortable limitations.

Let's take a moment now to create your own resilience inventory: a catalog of the strengths, wisdom, and survival tools that have carried you through difficult times. We often forget our own capabilities when we're in the middle of a crisis. Creating this inventory gives you tangible evidence of your capacity to overcome, something concrete to hold onto when everything feels uncertain.

Your resilience inventory should include both the gifts passed down through your family lineage and the strengths you've developed through your own experiences. Perhaps you inherited your grandmother's determined spirit or your father's pragmatic problem-solving. Maybe your cultural background equipped you with resourcefulness or community-building skills that have saved you time and again.

Having this inventory ready before crisis hits means you won't have to search for your strength when you're already depleted. It reminds you that difficulty isn't a sign you're doing something wrong—it's an opportunity to tap into resources you may have forgotten you possess. Your resilience inventory becomes a trusted foundation that supports you when everything else feels shaky.

Here are some questions you can use to start building it:

What stories of overcoming have been passed down in your family? Think about the stories of resilience you heard growing up—the relatives who survived wars, economic hardships, or personal tragedies. What qualities did they demonstrate that you might have inherited?

What trials have you already overcome that once seemed impossible? List specific challenges you've faced and how you navigated them.

What resources—internal and external—helped you through those times? Consider both personal strengths (determination, creativity, faith) and external supports (friends, community resources, spiritual practices).

What did those experiences teach you about your capacity for resilience? What did you learn about yourself that surprised you?

How did those trials ultimately expand you in ways you couldn't have anticipated? What unexpected gifts came from those difficult seasons?

Do you have a history of resilience to lean on and inherit as part of who you are? What family stories or cultural traditions remind you of your capacity to overcome?

Let me be clear that this inventory is not a record of your past; it's a resource for your future. When new trials come, you can draw on this evidence of your resilience.

It's important to remember that resilience requires trust. Trust that the breaking isn't the end of your story. Trust that your lowest moments are merely preparation for your highest ones. Trust that what feels like destruction is actually reconstruction.

Resilience is like a muscle—the more we rely on it, the stronger it gets. Each time we face a trial and choose to trust the process of transformation, our capacity for resilience expands. Like growing my mom's prized heirloom tomatoes, we learn to work with the weeds, weather, and pests that threaten the garden, transforming even the most challenging growing conditions into something beautiful and worth showing off at the end of the season.

Trusting your resilience is not saying, "Nothing bad will ever happen to me." It's believing that whatever happens, you'll find a way through it. It's the difference between blind optimism and hard-earned wisdom.

When you trust your resilience, you stop asking, "Am I strong enough for this?" and start asking, "How will I grow through this?" You stop seeing challenges as evidence that something's wrong with your life and start seeing them as evidence that your life is asking you to expand.

The beauty of resilience is that it compounds over generations. Each challenge we overcome makes us stronger while also creating a blueprint for those who come after us. I see it now in my own daughters, who carry within them the same fire that brought their grandmother across the ocean to build a new life.

My mother's favorite saying is, "You deal with the cards you're dealt." Simple words that carry weighted wisdom. Life isn't about waiting for perfect circumstances—it's about playing the hand you're given with grace and determination.

Take a moment to consider your present life circumstances that may be calling you to pull from your resilience inventory:

- What trial are you facing right now that you've been resisting rather than trusting? What might change if you viewed it as preparation rather than punishment?

- Where in your life are you creating unnecessary drama that's distracting you from the real growth trying to happen?

- What would change if you truly trusted that your trials were working to help you once you choose to use it for good?

- Where have you been asking "Why me?" when you could be asking "What for?"

Trust your resilience. It's been building for generations. It's in your DNA. It's in the stories of those who came before you and overcame impossible odds. It's in the way you've already survived what once seemed unsurvivable.

Your resilience isn't just about bouncing back. It's about moving forward. Every challenge you've faced has left you with wisdom, strength, and resources that weren't there before.

Your ancestor's strength runs in your veins. Your own victories speak to your capacity. Trust that. Trust yourself. The next storm isn't coming to break you—it's coming to reveal just how unbreakable you really are.

CHAPTER THREE

TRUSTING YOUR QUIRKS

"OH MY GOSH, YOU'RE SO TALL!"

If I had a dollar for every time I heard that growing up, I wouldn't have needed a career. At six feet tall by my teenage years, I towered over my classmates—especially the boys. My friends nicknamed me "Olive Oyl" after Popeye's gangly girlfriend, and while they meant it affectionately, it highlighted what I saw as my biggest flaw: being different.

Being a six-foot-tall teenage girl in small town Texas meant standing out when all I wanted was to blend in. While other girls my age were dating and being asked to dances, I was the one boys literally looked up to—and then quickly looked away from. At sixteen, I remember crying to my father about how no one would date me. His response, though frustrating at the time, held wisdom I wouldn't understand for years: "Do you want to have a lot of dates now, or later?"

What I couldn't see then was how the very things that made me feel different would become my greatest assets. Those long legs that made me feel awkward in high school would later carry me down runways. That height that made me stand out would help me stand up—not just physically, but in life.

But learning to see our differences as gifts rather than flaws? That took me years to figure out. And it started with understanding something fundamental about how we're designed: God made each of us with our own special combination of gifts.

I love how it says in the Bible that we're each given different talents, not to compete with each other, but so we can come together like a beautiful mosaic. I struggled with this for so long—I always looked up to my big sister since I wanted to be like her; looking at what other women had, and feeling like somehow I got the short end of the stick, which ironically stemmed from the height consciousness.

I've come to realize that when we compare ourselves to others, we're actually rejecting the unique path God designed for us. Your gifts won't look like mine, and mine won't look like yours—and that's the whole point. Your sister might be amazing with decorating cookies, while you might be amazing at dancing in the kitchen. Your friend might be an incredible athlete while you have this creative mind that sees possibilities others miss.

The world needs your specific combination of strengths, and yes, even your weaknesses. Because honestly? Sometimes the things we consider our weaknesses end up being the very qualities that make us effective in unexpected ways. My height made me self-conscious, but it also made me memorable. My openness about my struggles has sometimes been criticized as oversharing, but it's also created deeper connections with people who needed to know they weren't alone.

For far too long, I saw my differences as flaws to fix rather than gifts to develop. But your quirks aren't accidents —they're assignments. They're not random—they're purposeful. And they're not your weakness—they're your superpowers.

My first real taste of turning a perceived weakness into strength came during my seventh-grade year in cheerleading. I loved cheerleading with my whole heart, though I wasn't necessarily the best at it. A six-foot body isn't exactly built for back handsprings, but I was determined. My mother would drive me 45-60 minutes away for private lessons so I could master that one back handspring for tryouts. Yes, I'd do it once a year, that was it—but it was worth every minute of practice.

Then came the accident. I fell and hurt my hip—badly enough that I couldn't perform. Forced to sit on the sidelines for weeks, I did something that would later become a pattern in my life: I turned observation into opportunity. Instead of wallowing in self-pity, I began to study. I watched how the other girls moved, noted the sharpness of their motions, the height of their kicks, the precision of their jumps.

But I didn't just watch—I visualized. In my mind, I saw myself performing with that same grace and power.

I would envision exactly how I wanted my herkie to look, how high I wanted my toe touch to be. I didn't know it then, but I was practicing what athletes call mental rehearsal. Looking back now, I'm amazed that somehow, at such a young age, I knew to do this. Keep in mind that this was years ago before this concept of manifestation was as popular and widely understood as it is now. I didn't even know at the time that I was doing that. I just knew I wasn't going to sit there and not come out of this better on the other end. I was already possibly the worst of the eight girls, and I was determined to come back better.

When I finally healed and returned to the squad, something remarkable happened. All those hours of visualization translated into actual improvement. I became better than I'd been before the injury!

That experience taught me a lesson that would resurface again and again throughout my life: sometimes being sidelined is exactly what we need to grow.

Even when I couldn't perform physically, I could still trust my ability to grow and improve. I was learning to trust not just my body, but my mind, my determination, my ability to see myself differently than others saw me.

That pattern of turning setbacks into stepping stones should have built my confidence permanently. But life has a way of planting weeds of doubt in even the most minor moments.

I'll never forget an interaction with my seventh-grade math teacher. I had just failed a test, and as I sat there, trying to keep my tears from slipping down my cheeks, she walked over to me, patted my arm, and said, "Honey, don't worry, you'll get by on your looks in life."

I sat there, stunned. Even as a kid, I understood what she meant. She was telling me I wasn't smart, but it was okay because I had something else going for me. And that message—silent but loud—embedded itself somewhere deep inside me.

That moment was proof of how easily we can internalize other people's limitations of us. But here's what I wish I'd known then: just because someone else can't see your potential doesn't mean it's not there. Learning to trust your own assessment of yourself—that's where real confidence begins.

We all have those moments. A comment from a teacher, a family member, a peer, from another kid—small words that shape the way we see ourselves for years to come. And unless we recognize them for what they are, we carry them without even realizing it.

That's the danger of silent programming—those messages we absorb without questioning, whether we're seven or forty-seven. They slip in under our radar and start to color how we see ourselves and what we believe we're capable of. Maybe it was a parent who always compared you to a sibling, or a spouse who made subtle remarks that chipped away at your confidence. It could even be the things you tell yourself: "I'm not good with money," "I'm not the creative one," "I'll never be as successful as her." These messages build up, layer by layer, until we can't separate them from our own voice. And the scariest part? Most of the time, we don't even realize they're there, silently driving our decisions, our fears, our dreams, and even who we believe we are.

During high school, I ventured into modeling. At one go-see (what we called modeling interviews), I encountered the harsh realities of an industry that could be brutally critical. The moment crystalized the industry's demanding nature: a critique about my body that was both personal and impersonal. "We need to get rid of these," they said, pointing to my pointed hips, before quickly realizing as they touched them, "Oh, they're bones."

I was naturally thin—always had been—but apparently not the right kind of thin. I remember standing there, this tall girl who'd always felt a little "not enough" in so many ways: grades not high enough to make National Honor Society like most of my friends, not fast enough to win a gold medal in swim team like my bestie, not short enough to be desired by the boys. And now I was being told that even my bones—my actual skeleton—was somehow wrong. They wanted me to be a perfect hanger for clothes, not a woman with a natural human form, which was the image in the 90s.

What strikes me now is how casually they delivered these assessments, as if they were discussing a piece of furniture that needed refinishing rather than a young woman's body. The agent didn't even break eye contact or apologize when she realized she was critiquing something I literally couldn't change. She just moved on to the next critique, while I stood there trying to process how I could possibly "fix" my own bone structure.

It was my first real taste of an industry that could commodify and dissect a woman's body without a second thought. And though I didn't fully understand it then, these planted weeds of self-doubt would take years to recognize and uproot. How many times did I look in the mirror afterward and see "flaws" that were actually just natural human characteristics? How much mental energy did I waste trying to hide or minimize parts of myself that were perfectly fine just as they were?

Those experiences could have broken my confidence completely. Instead, I made a choice to let them strengthen my resolve, though the journey wasn't always straightforward.

I learned to distinguish between constructive feedback and destructive criticism. Constructive feedback helps you improve; destructive criticism tries to make you someone you're not. Learning to tell the difference—that's a skill that will serve you in every area of life.

What I began to realize was that the most successful individuals in any field aren't those who perfectly fit into a predetermined mold, but those who dare to stand out. In modeling, this became particularly clear. The industry might demand a certain standard, but it's the unique attributes that truly make a model memorable. Take Cindy Crawford's iconic mole, which she was once advised to remove but became her signature feature. Tyra Banks' fierce forehead and distinctive walk, Iman's regal bone structure that defied traditional Western beauty standards, or Kate Moss' unconventional petite frame—these were the very traits that set them apart in a sea of seemingly identical faces.

Success in any field isn't just about talent or appearance, but about the people you surround yourself with and your willingness to embrace what makes you different. The right support can transform even the most challenging experiences. In modeling, as in life, who you put yourself in the room with makes all the difference. Some might see the industry as having a negative connotation, but I learned that with the right perspective and the right people, even the most challenging environments can become opportunities for growth.

Over time, my height—once my greatest insecurity— became my greatest asset in the modeling world. What had made me feel awkward and out of place in school was precisely what made me valuable on the runway. The very thing I had tried to minimize by slouching and making myself smaller—the same thing that had hindered my cheerleading dreams—was now something to accentuate and celebrate.

Truth be told, for a lifetime, I downplayed the modeling part of my life, worried that people would think I was conceited or seeking attention because of how models can be perceived. I realized much later that this hesitation was about not fully trusting my own passions and God-given talents were mine for a reason, but I struggled embracing that. We do that, though, don't we? How often do we diminish our experiences, our successes, our desires, our unique paths because we're afraid of how others might perceive them?

This pattern of holding back, of trying to make ourselves smaller (sometimes literally in my case), often stems from early experiences where we learned that standing out wasn't safe or acceptable. But the very things that make us different are often the things that make us exceptional.

Our quirks often contain hidden gifts that reveal themselves precisely when we need them most. They're tools being sharpened for future use. That height that made me self-conscious? It taught me how to command a room in a male-dominated sales role. That sensitivity that made me feel so comfortable being vulnerable? It gave me the ability to connect deeply with others. That tendency to stand out? It taught me how to stand up for myself and others.

But the real test of trusting our quirks as superpowers comes not in the moments of success, but in the valleys of life.

All those experiences of feeling different were developing wisdom. When you're made fun of for being too tall, too sensitive, too enthusiastic, too quiet, too anything, you're learning something crucial about people and acceptance. When you struggle to fit in, you're developing empathy for others who feel like outsiders. When you notice things others miss, you're honing your unique perspective.

These experiences weren't just happening to you—they were forming you. They were creating insights that only you have, wisdom born from your specific combination of traits and experiences. And that wisdom? It deserves to be honored, especially by yourself.

EMBRACING YOUR UNIQUE EDGE

Think about it: How many times have you tried to shrink yourself—literally or figuratively—to fit in or to be accepted or meet expectations that aren't aligned with you? How often have you downplayed your unique qualities because you feared they made others uncomfortable? What if those very qualities are actually your superpowers in disguise? What if all your dreams could be reached when you learn how to use your quirks as your advantage and not as an obstacle?

Here are some questions to consider:

• What unique characteristic have you been trying to minimize that might actually be your greatest strength?

• How have your past experiences of feeling different prepared you for where you are now?

• What criticism have you received throughout your life that might actually point to your distinctive gift?

• Were there times of silent programming that you need to uncover and reframe?

• Where in your life are you still trying to blend in when you were created to stand out?

• What would change if you fully trusted your unique way of being in the world?

When I think about that teenage girl—feeling too tall, too different, too everything—I want to tell her something: "Trust this. Trust that these very things that make you feel different are actually preparing you for a life bigger than you can imagine."

Your quirks aren't mistakes in your design. They're not flaws to fix or obstacles to overcome. They're your assignment, your mission, your unique contribution to the world. The very thing that makes you feel different today might be exactly what someone else needs tomorrow.

In a world that often pushes for conformity, your quirks aren't just your superpowers—they're your signature. They're how people will remember you, how you'll make your mark, how you'll know you're living as your truest self.

So what superpower are you ready to stop hiding? What unique gift are you ready to trust enough to put on full display? Because the world is waiting for exactly what you have to offer—not in spite of your differences, but because of them.

PART TWO
WHEN TRUST IS BROKEN

CHAPTER FOUR

TRUSTING YOUR CHOICES

THE HARDEST PATTERNS TO RECOGNIZE THAT AFFECT TRUST ARE THE ones we're living inside. It took me decades to see how I had slowly, almost unnoticeably, taught myself to abandon who I really was. And yet, every single choice—every step, every yes—was shaping me into the woman I am today. I just didn't know it at the time.

Losing yourself doesn't happen overnight. It happens quietly, disguised as love, belonging, and safety. It happens when you want to make the people you care about proud— when you start making decisions that aren't really decisions at all, just repetitions of someone else's path.

For me, that path belonged to my very successful sister.

I didn't just follow in my oldest sister's footsteps; I lived inside her shadow, trusting her judgment and path more than my own. She went to this college, so I did too. She pledged this sorority, so I did too. She majored in speech communication, so I did too. She got a job in pharmaceutical sales, so I did too.

It didn't even feel like a choice although it was of

course. I fully trusted her judgment because it served her so well and ultimately served me well. She was successful in everything she did and always had been in my eyes. Oh, how I admired her, and she was the ultimate compass for me. Looking back, I can see how I was simply following a script—one that had already been written, tested, proven, and approved. It took out the question for me because I wanted to have the success she had.

But there's a difference between being guided by someone's wisdom but not having the confidence to trust your own inner compass.

The first time I really noticed how I abandoned my own compass was with my first serious relationship in high school.

I met him when I was sixteen. He was sweet, safe, steady. He came from a good family, respected his parents, and treated me well. He wasn't the guy who made my heart race, but he was kind, and in high school, that felt like enough.

Maybe part of me didn't think I could do better. Since I was so awkwardly tall, I wasn't the girl boys pursued. I was the friend. The one they joked around with, not the one they asked to dances. So when he showed interest, it felt like an invitation into something I wasn't sure that anyone else would invite me to.

And I stayed. For seven years. Even when I knew deep down that we weren't right for each other.

I stayed because it was easy. Because I didn't want to hurt him. Because he was a very nice guy. Because I didn't trust myself to want something more.

Then came the proposal. He had his family fly us to Key

West to stay in the family condo, and on the beach there, he asked me to marry him. And I said yes.

But something in me hesitated. I remember talking to his mom that night, telling her I felt uneasy. She said it was normal. And I believed her. I was so young, what did I know?

It wasn't excitement or nerves, though—it was something deeper, a knowing I wasn't ready to admit. But I ignored it. Because what kind of person walks away from a relationship that has no glaring flaws? What kind of person says, *I know this is fine, but fine isn't enough?*

Before I left for Italy to study abroad, I gave him back the ring—not as a break-up, but as a pause. "You keep it while I'm gone," I had said, not realizing that was my way of easing out of it, of slowly detaching.

Looking back, I can see the pattern so clearly. I had stayed in that relationship because I had abandoned so much of myself that I no longer knew how to want more.

I was afraid of hurting him. Afraid of disappointing him and his family. Afraid that maybe I couldn't do better. Afraid to trust my own instincts.

And that's another way we tend to lose ourselves— in the quiet patterns of deferring to others instead of listening to our own voice. We take the safer route, the proven path, the "good enough" relationship because forging our own way feels terrifying.

This is where I struggled most—trusting my own decisions. For years, I made choices based on what would please others, what would avoid conflict, what seemed safest. I didn't trust that I could make good decisions on my own— or more accurately, I didn't trust that decisions that served me were as valid as decisions that served others.

Think about it—how many choices have you made

primarily to avoid disappointing someone else? How many times have you ignored that quiet voice inside that whispered, "This isn't quite right for you," because speaking up felt too risky?

That's not to say we should make selfish decisions without considering others. But there's a difference between thoughtfully considering others and abandoning ourselves to please them. One comes from a place of strength and integrity; the other from fear and self-doubt.

When we consistently override our own needs and desires, we're teaching ourselves a dangerous lesson: that our voice doesn't matter, that our happiness is secondary, that our intuition can't be trusted. Each time we make choices from this place, we chip away at our connection to ourselves.

But here's the hopeful part: just as we can teach ourselves to doubt our decisions, we can also teach ourselves to trust them again. And sometimes, all it takes is one decision that comes from an authentic place—one choice that feels truly ours—to begin rebuilding that trust.

For me, that choice was Italy—the first thing I did differently than my family. It felt almost rebellious—and that felt kind of good. My sister had studied abroad in Spain and my family also had the desire for me to go to a Spanish-speaking country to follow my roots. If I had followed the script, I would have gone there, too, and it would have made sense. But sometimes your passion does not make sense.

When I arrived in Florence for my study abroad program, I thought I was ready. I had dreamed of this—living in Florence, immersing myself in the culture, traveling across Europe. But what I didn't anticipate was the immediate and overwhelming homesickness.

It hit me like a wave. The streets were foreign, the language was everywhere but nowhere I could grasp, and the little comforts of home—my Dodge Ram 2-door short-bed pickup, Walmart, Target, Texas chocolate sheet cake—felt a world away. I missed the familiar. I missed my routine. And most of all, I missed feeling like I *belonged*.

I had spent my whole life fitting in, but now, I was in a country where I was the foreigner. Even within my own group that I lived with, I felt different—I was the Southern girl among five East Coasters. Suddenly, my normal was no longer the majority. And that forced me to question: *Where do my values align? Where do they diverge?*

For the first few weeks, I floundered. I was caught between wanting to experience this grand adventure and feeling completely out of place. And then, something clicked. I realized I needed to stop waiting for someone else to make this experience meaningful for me. This was *my* journey—not my sister's, not my parents', not my Italian roommates'.

I sat down with my calendar and made a decision that would change everything: I would design my own experience. I mapped out weekends for travel, scheduled local cooking classes and museum visits, and committed to having daily coffee at the same café to create a sense of routine. For the first time, I wasn't following someone else's blueprint—I was creating my own.

I remember sitting in that small café, journaling about my plans, and feeling this surge of confidence. *I can do this my way. I don't need to do it like anyone else.* I was claiming my right to shape my own experience, to trust my own desires about what I wanted from this journey.

Journaling became my outlet. Every day, I wrote about

what I was seeing, learning, and feeling—both the excitement and the struggle. And as the months passed, I realized I was doing more than adjusting; I was *growing* into someone who could make decisions based on what I wanted, not what others expected of me.

I turned 21 in Italy. It was a year of stepping outside everything I knew, of realizing that I could build a life that looked different from what I had always expected. It taught me I could trust my ability to create my own path, even when it felt scary. Every time I made a decision based on what I truly wanted rather than what was expected, I was building trust in my own judgement, one small decision at a time.

The more I grew into myself in Italy, the more I realized how different my then fiancé and I were. I was becoming someone who craved adventure, who wanted to see the world, who was learning to trust herself in ways I never had before. And he? He didn't understand that. He didn't want that.

I wanted gnocchi with pesto and to grow and explore and experience new things; he was fine with corn dogs and grilled cheese and life as is. There's nothing wrong with either path—unless you're on the wrong one for you. I knew it was time to officially break up.

It was the first time I felt emboldened to really make decisions based on me, more than trying to please those around me.

FINDING MY OWN WAY

I've always been a natural connector. Even back in high school, they voted me "Most Friendly"—the one who could talk to anyone. This gift for connecting with people became one of my superpowers, though I didn't recognize it at the time.

After college, I landed what I thought was my dream job —assistant public relations manager at the Neiman Marcus flagship store. I mean, this was the epitome of everything I thought I wanted: my people skills combined with my love of fashion. I was hired literally two days after graduating, and I felt like I'd hit the jackpot.

But I only lasted three months.

First of all, my boss was basically "The Devil Wears Prada" in real life. But more importantly, I quickly realized the priorities of our customers didn't align with my farm-grown roots. I was an event planner for the store—organizing fashion shows and luncheons for the clientele—and I'd watch these women get genuinely upset about things like the color of the bows on their gift bags being slightly wrong.

I remember thinking, "Oh my gosh, this is just not who I am." This obsession with perfection felt so foreign to me. When you've been raised with stories about your family escaping Cuba and starting over with nothing, it's hard to get worked up about color-coordinated ribbons.

So I left. And looking back, what's interesting is how quickly I interpreted that experience as a personal failure.

Don't get me wrong—I don't regret that career or want to diminish it at all. It was a tough job to get! I worked my butt off for six months to land that position at possibly the top department store in the country, and I was so proud. It provided for me and taught me so much.

But it's fascinating how I let that little "failure" at Neiman's derail me from finding my own way. One small detour, and I immediately abandoned trust in my own direction. That's how fragile our self-trust can be sometimes —and how easily we can lose sight of who we really are when faced with challenges.

The "what now?" question haunted me. I studied speech communication with a minor in fashion—not exactly a clear career path.

As I mentioned, my oldest sis was my greatest mentor— showing me what was possible, opening doors I never knew existed. We formed a badass team. My sister was already thriving in pharmaceutical sales. She'd always been my north star.

"You should try pharmaceutical sales," she told me. "You'd be great at it."

At first, I worried I wasn't smart enough. I mean, these pharma reps talk to doctors all day—actual physicians with medical degrees! I'd never been a science person. School didn't come easy for me. I wasn't the academic type who could memorize medical terminology without breaking a sweat.

But what I did understand was people.

My first territory included both upscale medical centers and rural clinics. I remember walking into my first meeting with this renowned cardiologist who had a reputation for being impossible—he'd kicked more pharmaceutical reps out of his office than anyone in the district.

I was terrified. But then something clicked: I didn't need to be the smartest person in the room. I just needed to be authentic.

I developed my own approach over those thirteen years. While other reps focused on memorizing every scientific detail, I focused on building relationships. I'd ask the office staff about their kids. I remembered nurses' birthdays. I brought homemade cookies to offices during the holidays.

One day, my district manager rode along with me on calls. After our third appointment, he looked at me curiously.

"You know," he said, "most reps spend 80% of their time talking about the product and 20% building rapport. You do the opposite—and it is amazing how it opens doors others can't open."

I just smiled. "People don't buy from companies. They buy from people they trust."

This wasn't always smooth sailing. There were plenty of times I felt inadequate, especially at national sales meetings when others would discuss complex drug mechanisms that made my eyes glaze over. I'd sit there thinking, "Am I smart enough to do this?" But then I'd get my quarterly numbers, and there I'd be—in the top ten percent.

In rural clinics, I'd dress differently—more casual, approachable. I'd talk about my family's farm, finding common ground. With the university doctors, I'd be more formal but still authentic. I learned to read a room, to adapt without losing myself. I was being respectful of different environments while staying true to my core values.

It was validation that trusting my instincts—even when they differed from what everyone else was doing—was the right call. I was still following my sister's career path, but I was walking it in my own shoes.

That's where so many of us get stuck. We see someone else's success and try to carbon-copy their methods instead of adapting them to our unique strengths. I wasn't going to out-science the science majors, but I could out-connect anyone.

And here's the thing: it worked. I excelled in that role for thirteen years. I was good at it. I built a successful career, won awards, hit my sales goals, and created a life that looked, on paper, like the definition of achievement.

But success that isn't rooted in true passions eventually comes at a cost. You'll start to feel it within your bones, and that's when you know it's time for a change.

LEARNING TO TRUST YOUR CHOICES

So here's what I want to say, looking back on it all: *Trust every single thing you've said yes to.*

Even the things that didn't turn out how you expected. Even the relationships that ended. Even the choices that seemed like missteps.

Because those yeses—every single one—shaped you into who you are. And instead of carrying regret, what if you carried gratitude? Gratitude for the lessons. Gratitude for the experiences. Gratitude for the moments that forced you to grow, even when you didn't want to.

Take a moment to reflect on:

- Where in your life have you followed someone else's path instead of your own? What were you afraid would happen if you chose differently?

- Have you ever felt a deep knowing about a choice but ignored it? What happened, and what did you learn?

- What choices have shaped you the most, even if

they didn't turn out the way you expected? What gifts came from those "wrong" turns?

- How has fear played a role in the decisions you've made? Where can you replace that fear with trust?

- When have you felt most alive and authentic? What were you doing differently in those moments?

You have never been off-track. You have never made a decision that God didn't already know how to use. Every step, every season, every moment—it's all been part of your path.

So instead of questioning where you've been, start trusting where you are.

The next time you feel that quiet whisper that says, there's more...

Trust it.

The next time you feel a nudge to step in a direction that feels both terrifying and right...

Trust it.

The next time you hear yourself say, "I don't know if I can do this"...

Trust that you can.

Because you are already exactly where you are supposed to be. And you are being led to exactly where you need to go.

CHAPTER FIVE

TRUSTING WHEN IT'S TIME
FOR A CHANGE

AT FIRST, WHEN THAT RESTLESS FEELING HIT, I TRIED TO IGNORE IT.

I had a stable career, a clear trajectory. My father, being the traditional physician he was, couldn't understand why I would consider ever leaving pharmaceutical sales. "That's a stable thing," he'd say. "Why would you leave a stable thing?"

I didn't have an answer for him at the time. I just knew something inside me was restless.

I would hear other people talk about their work with passion, excitement, fire—and I started to wonder why I didn't feel the same way. I wasn't miserable. I was just... disconnected. Like I was moving through the motions of a life that had been perfectly curated, but not one I had chosen for myself. And that's the tricky thing about following a proven path—it doesn't feel *wrong* enough to question. But if you're not careful, it becomes a slow erosion of self-trust.

Because the truth was, my real gifts weren't being used. I'd been craving something of my own business-wise for

years. I considered opening a bridal shop—I love fashion—
or maybe a bakery. But fear kept stopping me. Fear of the
hours, fear of the overhead, fear of time away from my
family as a mother.

My superpowers weren't in following a script. They
were in building relationships, connecting with people,
creating authentic bonds—not just selling a product, but
making people feel seen, heard, and valued.

In 2008, my sister randomly introduced me to this direct
sales jewelry company she'd heard about. "You've always
wanted something for yourself," she told me. "You should
look into this."

I completely ignored her. In my head, I'm thinking, "My
God, I'm way too busy for something like that!"

But my sister kept mentioning this jewelry company
opportunity over the span of three or four weeks. Finally,
she decided to try it herself. Houston had just been hit with
a disaster, and her entrepreneurial income had declined
overnight because her clients were spending less. She
thought, "I'll supplement my income a little with this
jewelry thing."

A few days later, I went to her house and saw the
jewelry. "Oh my, it's so cute!" I said. She gave me that look
—"I've been telling you to check this out, and you've been
ignoring me!"

Something clicked, and I thought, "Maybe I'll try this."
But I was still fearful. What if I looked like that crazy direct
sales lady? I didn't want to be "that person" who wasn't
respected for what they chose to do. All those typical fears
were washing through me.

But I decided to jump in anyway. My younger sister and
I joined her about two weeks after she started. In that short

time, we could already see her having tremendous success. She had more time to focus on building the business than we did since my younger sister and I were still accountable to our corporate jobs. I kept thinking, "If I just had more time..."

I started following the training, and I had immediate success—not because I'm great, but because I'm very coachable. I learned that word about myself during this time and saw it become one of my greatest strengths.

Then I got mono from trying to burn the candle at both ends—trying to learn this business (that I didn't even realize I was starting), working my full-time job, being a mom, and helping my husband-at-the-time run his practice. My body was exhausted. Something had to give.

That illness was the boulder that shook up my life. It made me realize I had to make a choice. Do I choose comfort and so-called "security" with benefits and a paid-for car in a full-time corporate job? Or do I choose the endless expansion and opportunity within myself?

I chose option two. I leaned in. I knew that if I followed the training and did what successful people in that industry do, I could do it too.

We worked with our budget and figured out that in the first month, I needed to make $1,500 minimum to cover our health insurance and my car payment, since my then husband was self-employed and we got our insurance through my company.

So I intentionally filled my calendar with exactly how it needed to be to generate the business I needed going forward. And that first month? I made at least that amount, if not a little more. And I never made less after that.

I made a decision. I trusted myself. I went forward.

Looking back, that boulder—getting so sick that I couldn't keep doing everything—was actually a gift. It forced me to trust myself in a way I never had before. It pushed me to stop hedging my bets and commit fully to something I believed in. And every time I hit my income goals, it was like my intuition saying, "See? I told you it was time for a change. I told you this was the right choice."

Sometimes the universe has to knock us down a bit before we're willing to stand up in a new direction. For me, that illness was a redirect toward the business that would eventually change everything for me. It taught me that trusting yourself isn't just about having blind faith—it's about taking that first leap, then showing up consistently to prove that your intuition was right all along.

I had spent so much of my life trusting other people's paths that I had never trusted myself to create my own. And the irony? The very qualities that I thought made me a follower—my relational nature, my deep empathy, my ability to connect with people—were the exact qualities that made me successful once I stepped into leadership.

I used to think that leadership meant being the loudest voice in the room, having all the answers, demanding authority. But that wasn't me.

What was me?

Being relational.

Building deep trust with people.

Making sure others felt supported and empowered.

And it turns out, that's leadership too.

KNOWING WHEN IT'S TIME

Take a moment to reflect on your own journey of recognizing when it's time for a change:

- Where in your life are you feeling restless or disconnected? What might that be telling you?

- What passions or gifts have you been ignoring out of fear or practicality? How might you start honoring them?

- Think about a time when you took a leap of faith and trusted yourself to make a change. What did you learn about yourself in that process?

- What qualities or strengths do you possess that could make you a great leader, even if they don't fit the traditional mold?

- What would be possible in your life if you trusted yourself to create your own path?

Remember, recognizing when it's time for a change isn't about abandoning everything you've built. It's about having the courage to listen to that inner voice that's telling you *there's more*—more alignment, more fulfillment, more impact.

The path to your purpose isn't always a straight line. Sometimes it involves detours, unexpected turns, and leaps of faith. But every step is preparing you for the moment when you finally trust yourself to create your own way.

So the next time you feel that restlessness, that longing for something more? Pay attention. It's not a distraction from your purpose—it might just be the very thing that leads you to it.

Trust the journey. Trust the timing. But most of all? Trust yourself. Because the world needs the leader you were born to be—and that leader is already inside you, just waiting for you to say yes.

CHAPTER SIX

TRUSTING AFTER TRUST IS SHATTERED

TRUST IS LIKE A MIRROR. ONCE IT'S BROKEN, YOU CAN TRY TO PIECE it back together, but the cracks will always be there. At least, that's what I used to think. What I've learned is that sometimes, broken trust is actually an invitation to build something completely new, something even stronger than before. But to get there, you've got to be willing to wade through the wreckage first.

I met Steve in a bar in Dallas. He was playing bass in the band, totally lost in his music the way musicians do. He caught my eye right away—handsome, dark-haired, intense. But my first thought? Gosh, he's too short. (The struggles of being a tall girl!)

My friend, a few drinks in, decided to play cupid and marched right up to tell him I wanted to meet him. I was so embarrassed. Talking to people was easy for me, especially after being in medical sales, but flirting? That just wasn't my thing.

Still, the moment we started talking, something just clicked.

His eyes drew me in, and the way he carried a conversation—it wasn't just small talk, but the kind of discussion that made me feel like I was the only person in the world. I've always had a thing for creative, artistic types, maybe because it was such a contrast to my own conservative upbringing.

Steve had gone to college, but he had chosen to pursue music instead. Traveling with the band, living a life that seemed so foreign to the structured one I was used to. There was something I really admired about that—having the courage to chase a dream instead of following a traditional path.

When my roommate suggested he come back to our place after the show, I gave her a look that said, "Are you crazy? He's in a band!" But he did come over, and we ended up talking until the sun came up.

You know what really stood out to me? He never even took his shoes off.

That small detail stuck with me then, and it still does now. To me, it was proof that he was different from the stereotype, proof that he was respectful, proof that I could trust him. And I did trust him, completely. I was head over heels, and he seemed to feel the same way about me.

For the first ten years of our marriage, anyone who saw us would have told you how much he adored me. Even at the end, I believe that was still true.

But love alone isn't enough.

Over the course of our 23-year marriage, small things started to chip away at the trust we had built—not all at once, but gradually, persistently. Hidden decisions made without discussion. Dismissive reactions when I'd express concerns, making me feel like I was overreacting to things that genuinely worried me. A growing sense that my values and my need for security just weren't being considered in choices that affected our whole family.

At first, they were like tiny cracks in a mirror—easy to overlook, easier to explain away. *Maybe he's just stressed. Maybe I'm being too sensitive. Maybe this is just how marriage works.* But they kept happening, and I kept trying to fix what I thought was broken communication rather than recognizing a fundamental misalignment on what a partnership is.

I tried to address these issues, more times than I can count. For years, I would bring up my concerns, hoping that talking about it would change things. I'd suggest we make decisions together that affect the family. I'd ask for transparency about purchases that affected our budget. I'd express how certain actions made me feel unheard or unvalued. Each time, I'd walk away from those conversations believing we'd reached an understanding that things would be different going forward.

But I couldn't bring myself to fully trust my own intuition, which was screaming that something was fundamentally wrong. The pattern would repeat—the same dismissive responses, the same hidden choices, the same feeling that my input didn't really matter. And each time, instead of trusting that inner voice that was trying to protect me, I'd tell myself I must not be explaining myself clearly enough, or that I needed to be more patient, or that this was just a rough patch we'd work through.

I spent years trying to fix something that wasn't actually a communication problem—it was a respect problem. But I couldn't see that then. I just kept hoping that if I loved harder, supported more, explained better, somehow the foundation would stop cracking.

Instead, those tiny cracks kept spreading, slowly wearing away at the very foundation of our partnership, until the day I could no longer ignore what my intuition had been trying to tell me all along.

It was a cold November night. Late. I was lying in bed with that familiar, nagging unrest—the kind that settles in your chest and refuses to let you sleep. I had prayed this prayer before, more times than I could count.

"Lord, just tell me what to do."

And then, I heard it—not audibly, but in that way where you just know it's not your own thought.

"Go and find the truth."

My heart started racing. Was this God speaking to me? Or was I losing my mind? For thirty minutes, I wrestled with this prompting, lying there in the dark alone. My husband was asleep in the garage apartment because we had been so disconnected. Was this voice divine guidance or was I being tormented by doubt and suspicion? The voice was so clear, so insistent, but what if I was wrong? What if this was just my anxiety spiraling out of control?

Am I crazy? I kept asking myself. *Is this really something I need to act on, or am I creating problems where none exist?*

The nudge wouldn't go away. It felt urgent, almost desperate, like a warning I couldn't ignore. But acting on it would mean getting dressed at 2:00 in the morning, driving to his office, and searching for... what? I had no idea what I was looking for. I just knew I had to go.

My hands were shaking as I put on clothes. Every

rational thought screamed at me to go back to bed, to stop being paranoid, to trust instead of investigate. But there was something deeper than rational thought driving me—an inner knowing that felt both terrifying and necessary.

The drive to his office felt like the longest ten minutes of my life. My mind raced with possibilities: *What if I find nothing and I've completely lost it? What if I find something and my whole world falls apart? What if this voice I'm following isn't God but my own insecurity turned destructive?*

I sat in the parking lot for several minutes, engine running, trying to discern the difference between intuition and insanity.

But the nudge was so persistent, so clear. *Go and find the truth.*

So I got out of the car and followed that inner voice, my hands shaking, my breath uneven. Deep down, I already knew what I was about to discover. My intuition had been trying to tell me for months, maybe years. Tonight was just the night I finally had the courage to listen.

And there it was on his computer. Undeniable evidence of a breach of trust that I could no longer rationalize away, ignore, or explain. The truth I had been avoiding was right there in front of me, heartbreaking and impossible to deny.

In that moment, I felt so many things all at once. Shock, disbelief, a desperate wish to turn back time. But most of all, I felt an overwhelming sense of relief. Relief that I wasn't losing my mind, that my instincts had been right all along, even though I had tried so hard not to see it.

All at once, years of doubts, of rationalizing away my own discomfort, of ignoring my gut feelings to preserve the image of our life together, it all came crashing down around me. Suddenly, the past looked completely different, every memory tainted by the truth I had refused to acknowledge.

I realized that I had spent so long trying to be the perfect partner, the understanding wife, that I had completely betrayed my own instincts. I had seen all the warning signs, felt them deep in my bones, but I had chosen to overlook them because I was so afraid of what I might lose.

In the aftermath, I was in a kind of pain I had never experienced before. I doubted everything—my judgment, my desirability, my worth. How could I trust myself when I had been so wrong about something so basic?

Knowing that the violation of trust was going on during my cancer was perhaps the cruelest twist of all. Life has a way of layering challenges that force you to dig deeper than you ever thought possible. Just when you think you've survived the worst thing that could happen, something else comes along that tests every ounce of strength you thought you'd already spent.

The timing made me question everything about myself in the most brutal way. But that's what betraying trust does —it makes you absorb blame that was never yours to carry. The reality is that someone else's choices during my most vulnerable time said nothing about my worth. Learning to separate my value from someone else's actions became as crucial to my healing as any formal treatment could ever be.

It was through therapy that I gradually started to understand that my reactions were a normal response to a very abnormal situation. I wasn't crazy; I was a survivor of betrayal trauma. The person who was supposed to be my safe haven had become the source of my pain. It's no wonder my mind and body were struggling to cope.

Coming to understand this was a turning point for me. It

allowed me to start extending compassion to myself, to recognize that my intuition had never been wrong; I had just learned to stop trusting it.

Healing from betrayal is messy, it's repetitive, and it's different for everyone. There's no set timeline, no definitive endpoint, no instruction manual. But there is hope.

Looking back, I can see now that the betrayal wasn't just his—it was mine, too. The greatest heartbreak wasn't the trust I had put in him, but the trust I had failed to put in myself.

I'm not going to lie, it was hard. There were days when I questioned every move I made, nights when I cried myself to sleep, wondering if I would ever feel whole again. But little by little, even when I could barely see it at first, I started to heal.

I learned that trust isn't something you give once and then forget about. It's an everyday practice, a deliberate choice to listen to your deepest intuition. It's a muscle you have to keep strengthening, a garden you have to keep tending.

More than anything, I'm learning to give myself the same grace, compassion, and unconditional love that I used to reserve only for others. I'm learning to trust myself first, to be my own best friend, my own biggest advocate.

If you're going through something similar, I want you to know this: you're not alone. Your pain is real, your instincts are trustworthy, and your healing is possible. Having our trust violated can break us, but it can also be the beginning of our most powerful transformation.

It starts with being willing to sit with the discomfort, to face the pain head-on, to trust that your heartbreak isn't the end of your story, but the beginning of a much more beautiful one.

A story of resilience. Of rediscovering yourself. Of building a trust in your own being that can never be taken from you again.

That's the story I'm living now. And it's the story I believe you can live, too.

Because on the other side of betrayal, there's a strength you never knew you had. A love for yourself that you never thought was possible. A trust in who you are that can weather any storm.

And let me tell you, that is worth fighting for.

FINDING YOUR WAY BACK TO TRUST

The question I'm asked most often when I share my story is, "How do you ever trust again after something like that?"

It's a good question. Trust doesn't just magically reappear after betrayal. It has to be deliberately, intentionally rebuilt—starting with yourself.

First, I Had to Trust Myself Again

Before I could ever trust another person, I had to rebuild trust with myself. This meant:

- Acknowledging where I had ignored my intuition
- Forgiving myself for not seeing warning signs sooner
- Developing practices that strengthened my connection to my inner knowing

• Setting boundaries that honored my needs and values
• Celebrating moments when I did trust myself, even in small ways

I also practiced small acts of self-trust daily. When something felt wrong, I would pause and ask: "What am I feeling right now? Where is this feeling coming from?"

I started acknowledging my emotions without labeling them as "too much" or "too dramatic." I validated my own experiences without needing outside confirmation. And I set boundaries based on what felt right to me, not what others expected

My therapist suggested creating an "evidence list" of all the times my intuition had been right throughout my life. This list became concrete proof that I could trust myself, that my perceptions were accurate, that my inner guidance system worked.

I Learned the Difference Between Discernment and Suspicion

There's a big difference between being discerning and being suspicious. Suspicion assumes the worst without evidence. Discernment observes patterns and makes assessments based on actual behavior over time.

I had to learn that being careful wasn't the same as being closed. I could open my heart to new relationships while still paying attention to how people showed up in my life. I could give people the chance to earn my trust without blindly giving it away.

. . .

I Started Small

After betrayal, we often swing between extremes: trusting no one or desperately wanting to trust someone completely to prove we're "healed." Neither serves us well.

I learned that healthy trust builds gradually. I started by trusting people with small things before trusting them with bigger ones. I watched for consistency between their words and actions. I noticed how they responded when I expressed needs or set boundaries.

When I began dating again, I paid attention to things like: Did they show up when they said they would? How promptly and consistently did they respond to messages, and did they proactively communicate? Did they share appropriately about themselves, or overshare in ways that felt like false intimacy? Were they consistent in how they treated me from one meeting to the next?

These observations helped me gauge whether someone was trustworthy before I invested deeply in the relationship.

I Distinguished Between Different Types of Trust

After my divorce, I realized trust isn't monolithic. I was blessed with deep, reliable relationships with my sisters and an incredible group of lifelong friends who had proven their loyalty over decades. These connections remained unshaken.

What I lost wasn't trust in everyone—it was trust in a particular kind of relationship. My experience hadn't taught me to doubt all men; after all, I had wonderful examples in my two brother-in-laws who demonstrated what committed, honest partnerships looked like. Instead, I needed to rebuild my understanding of trust within romantic intimacy.

This distinction became crucial to my healing. Rather than seeing trust as something I needed to rebuild entirely, I recognized that I already knew how to trust wisely in many contexts. I could draw on those strengths while developing new discernment specifically for romantic relationships. This perspective allowed me to approach dating with hope rather than fear, knowing I wasn't starting from scratch but rather applying well-developed skills to a new domain.

I Deepened My Faith

As a woman of faith, the most significant healing in my trust journey came through leaning on God's faithfulness. This wasn't about putting a shiny bow on pain or using overused feel-good clichés. I wasn't interested in spiritual-izing away the hurt or offering myself empty platitudes. This was about raw, authentic connection with God in the midst of brokenness.

Throughout this journey, I've continued to find comfort in my lifelong scripture, Isaiah 41:10 (NKJV): "Fear not, for I am with you." In my darkest moments, these words became my anchor. They reminded me that I wasn't navigating this wilderness alone—God was with me, guiding me, some-times even pushing me toward truths I wasn't looking for and didn't want to find.

When my intuition was screaming that something wasn't right, when doors kept opening to reveal what was really happening in my marriage, I heard that gentle whis-per: "Fear not, I'm leading you." The evidence that landed in my hands wasn't coincidental—it was divine guidance confirming what my heart had known all along.

I also found comfort in Romans 8:28: "And we know that in all things God works for the good of those who love him, who have been called according to his purpose." This didn't mean the violation of trust itself was good. It meant God could work through even this deepest pain to create something beautiful in and through me—not despite my brokenness, but because of how that brokenness opened me to deeper healing.

When trust is shattered—especially when we ignore red flags along the way—it can feel impossible to rebuild. But that rebuilding starts with acknowledging that our intuition was never wrong. We weren't foolish; we were hopeful. We weren't blind; we were trying. And now, we have the opportunity to honor what we felt all along.

There comes a point in healing after betrayal when you realize that you are separate from the circumstances that broke you. That the actions of another person do not define you. That you are not at fault for loving someone who didn't handle that love well. And that's when the release happens.

The release is trusting that even though I didn't listen to my intuition then, I can learn from it now. That every ignored feeling, every buried warning sign, every moment of self-doubt was actually an opportunity to grow in trust— real trust. Not in another person, but in myself.

Because the truth is, I wasn't wrong to feel uneasy. I wasn't wrong to question. I wasn't wrong to notice the small things that didn't add up. And neither are you. If you've ever felt like you failed yourself by not seeing the truth sooner, let me tell you this: You didn't fail. You learned. And now you get to trust yourself even more deeply.

Take some time to reflect on your own journey with trust and betrayal:

- Have you ever ignored a red flag because facing it would have meant making a difficult decision? What did that cost you?

- When was the last time your intuition tried to warn you? Did you listen? What happened?

- Where have you been blaming yourself for someone else's choices? How might self-forgiveness play a role in your healing?

- What small act of self-trust could you practice today? (It might be as simple as honoring a boundary or acknowledging a feeling without judgment.)

- What evidence do you have from your past that your intuition is trustworthy? Make your own "evidence list."

- What would it look like to rebuild trust in yourself after it's been shattered?

The past may have shaped us, but it does not define our

future. What defines us is what we choose to do with the lessons we've learned. And I choose trust—trust in myself, trust in my voice, trust that I will never again ignore what I was meant to hear and see all along.

And you can too.

CHAPTER SEVEN

TRUSTING ADVERSITY AS A STRENGTH TRAINER

"KEEP ME OUT OF THE DARKNESS."

Those were the first words I prayed, lying on that cold exam table in 2017 when I heard the words no one ever wants to hear: "You have breast cancer." It wasn't a carefully thought-out prayer. It wasn't shaped by years of biblical study. It was instinct, a desperate plea from deep inside me. And yet, almost immediately, a calm, clear voice inside me responded: *I can do this. It's going to be okay.*

In that moment, I chose hope—which, as I'd later learn from Oprah, is viral. It spreads faster than fear if you let it.

Before we dive into my cancer story, I want to share something I've discovered through my journey that's completely changed how I view adversity. Adversity isn't one-size-fits-all, and neither is the strength it builds. Some storms come with built-in support systems—caring communities, meals delivered to your door, cards flooding your mailbox. Others force you to stand alone, to rely on nothing but God and your own resilience. Both build different muscles, and both, I've learned, are essential.

Just like there are different types of physical training that build different muscles, there are three distinct types of adversity that build different kinds of strength.

Some adversity is about **endurance**—persevering through sustained challenges, not sprinting through a crisis but pacing yourself for a marathon. Other challenges are about **resistance**—like pushing against weights at the gym, these come when external forces try to define, limit, or break you down. And sometimes adversity demands **flexibility**— requiring that you bend without breaking, adapting to a completely new reality.

Understanding which type of strength training you're facing doesn't make it easier, but it does help you approach it with the right mindset and tools. Let me share how these played out in my life, so you can recognize them in yours— and there's no better way to do this than to give you insight into the triple threat storm that helped me understand this best.

Endurance Training: Cancer and the Long Road

When I went through cancer, I discovered the hardest challenges aren't always the ones that look the most devastating on paper. Yes, cancer was terrifying. But I was wrapped in a cocoon of love and support. My eight-year-old daughter would FaceTime her best friend, confidently declaring, "Mom's going to be fine. They're just going to do the surgery, and then she'll be all better." Her certainty, born from my own displayed confidence, nearly brought me to tears. The way we face our challenges doesn't just affect us —it ripples out, touching everyone around us.

But here's what I learned about endurance training

through cancer: it's not like other challenges that have clear end dates. This wasn't something that would be over in a few weeks or even months. Even when—*if*—I hit remission, cancer would always be part of my story. It would live in the back of my mind during every future scan, every unexplained ache, every annual checkup. Endurance training means accepting that some challenges become permanent companions rather than temporary visitors.

As I was going through my cancer treatment, there was this day I was supposed to get an MRI, and I was nervous about what the results would show. You know how that feels—when you're waiting for something that could change everything.

If you recall from chapter two, that morning while getting ready, I put on my wedding ring, which had the stone from my mother's first wedding ring. Then I added my wedding band, which was actually my grandmother's wedding band. I mean, I had another band I could've worn —it was stronger and newer than my grandmother's—but something made me reach for hers that day.

I remember thinking, "I'm just going to wrap myself in the strength of these women that have preceded me," like I could somehow lean into their example of resilience and courage. I needed to feel them with me that day—to remind myself I come from women who've faced impossible things and kept going.

Every single day during treatment, I journaled one question: *What am I meant to learn from this day?* And every single day at the radiation center, I would make it a priority to connect with someone and learn more about them.

It wasn't about positivity—it was about purpose. Even on the hard days. *Especially* on the hard days.

I don't know if someone gave me that idea, or if it was divine guidance, but it became my lifeline during treatments. It helped me see where there was a greater purpose, where possibly through this challenge, God was leading me to something beyond the pain. Maybe it was connecting with somebody in the waiting room, helping someone else through their journey, or learning something from them that would help me grow. These encounters and reflections revealed little aspects of why this might be happening—because there's always a greater purpose to what we're going through than just the pain, turmoil, and hurt, if we're willing to look for it.

This practice helped me make sense of things. It gave me direction when I felt completely untethered. And more than anything, it reinforced a truth I hadn't fully embraced before: breaking isn't failing.

Cancer taught me endurance isn't about never getting tired; it's about finding the courage to rest and then continue. It's not about maintaining the same pace every day; it's about adjusting your expectations based on what your body and spirit can handle at this moment, on this day.

When facing endurance challenges, the key questions to ask yourself are:

• How can I pace myself for the long haul?

• What small daily rituals will keep me connected to hope?

• Where can I find meaning even in the difficult days?

• How can I celebrate small victories along the way?

Endurance adversity builds patience, perseverance, and perspective—qualities that will serve you in every area of life long after the immediate challenge has passed.

· · ·

Resistance Training: The Lawsuit That Changed Everything

Just as I was completing my cancer treatments, I faced an entirely different kind of adversity—one that would test me in ways cancer never did.

My sisters and I had built something incredible within a direct sales jewelry company—the company I had transitioned into after years of working in pharmaceutical sales. It started as something fun, an extra stream of income, but within a few years, my sisters and I were responsible for thousands of stylists. I had helped coach, mentor, and empower so many women to build their own businesses. I put a full decade into my work there.

And in those months of chemo and recovery, my team at work showed up for me. The same women I had spent years supporting in business lifted me up. They cheered me on, sent me messages, and created t-shirts to show me support. I felt like I belonged to something bigger than myself, like I was part of a community that truly cared.

But not all storms come with casseroles and care packages.

Right before my cancer treatments ended, the ground had already started shifting beneath me. The company that had once felt like home was changing. Big, corporate-driven changes. The kind that prioritized profit over people. The kind that made us—leaders with a decade of loyalty—start to question the direction things were headed.

And we weren't alone in that. Other top leaders were feeling it too.

The company was shifting its entire business model. The core compensation plans were changing, the way we built our businesses was changing, and decisions were being made that we strongly disagreed with. It no longer aligned with the business we had worked so hard to build.

And then came the offer.

Another jewelry company—a direct competitor—saw what we had built and wanted us to bring our leadership and our vision to them. They weren't just promising better compensation or a more stable structure; they were promising alignment with what we believed in.

It wasn't a decision we took lightly. We prayed about it. We wrestled with it. We researched for weeks. We weighed the risks.

But ultimately, my sisters and I decided to leave.

Our former company did not take it well. Within days of our departure, whispers started. False narratives spread. Then came the lawsuit—a full-scale legal attack against us.

Now we weren't just leaving—we were being *punished* for leaving.

The emotional toll was immense. I would sit at my kitchen table staring at legal documents, wondering how we had gone from building a company with integrity to defending ourselves in courtrooms.

I remember telling my sisters, "This lawsuit is worse than cancer." They looked at me like I was crazy, but one day, people are praying over you; the next, they're whispering about you and will not be seen in social photos with you.

What made this so different from cancer was the nature of the opposition itself. With cancer, I was fighting alongside my medical team toward a shared goal—remission. But with the lawsuit, I was fighting against deliberate forces that seemed determined to paint us as something we weren't. We wanted vindication, we wanted our reputation restored, we wanted the truth to prevail—but at every turn, we faced calculated resistance designed to wear us down.

This wasn't about enduring a long journey with a supportive community cheering us on. This was about standing firm when external forces were actively trying to move us from our position, to make us doubt our own integrity, to pressure us into admitting fault where we felt none existed.

That's when I learned that resistance training builds different muscles than endurance does. It teaches you to:

• Hold your ground when external forces try to move you
• Distinguish between battles worth fighting and those to walk away from
• Maintain your integrity when others question it
• Find strength in standing alone when necessary

When facing resistance challenges, the key questions to ask yourself are:

• What truth am I being called to stand firm in?
• How can I respond rather than react to opposition?
• What boundaries do I need to establish or maintain?
• Where can I find the courage to face this opposition?

Resistance adversity builds courage, conviction, and clarity—qualities that will help you navigate conflict and stand in your truth even when it's uncomfortable.

Flexibility Training: When Divorce Demands Adaptation

And then, another storm hit: the end of my marriage.

People say everything comes in threes, and within three years, cancer, a lawsuit, and divorce all reshaped my life.

Twenty-three years of what I thought was my story suddenly read like fiction. I remember standing in my kitchen, gripping the counter, sobbing. Now the ground beneath me didn't just feel shaky—it felt like it had disappeared altogether. When you realize so much of what you believed was built on lies, how do you trust anything?

For a long time, I didn't give myself permission to process it. I felt guilt-ridden, as if falling apart meant I had failed somehow. I kept pushing forward, trying to prove I was okay, trying to stay strong. But here's the thing: *you can't heal what you won't let yourself feel*. Breaking isn't the enemy—denying the breaking is.

It's interesting. Cancer didn't make me question my worth. Divorce did. Cancer didn't make me feel like my entire past was a lie. Divorce did. Cancer patients get casseroles. Divorce survivors often face judgment or uncomfortable silence—and the disorienting realization that years of their life may not have been what they seemed.

Flexibility training is perhaps the most uncomfortable of all adversities because it requires letting go of who you thought you were to become who you're meant to be. It's about adapting to a completely new reality—sometimes one you never asked for or wanted.

What made divorce so challenging wasn't just losing my marriage; it was losing my identity as a wife, my understanding of my past, my vision for my future, and even my trust in my own perceptions. Everything I thought I knew had to be reexamined.

But in that painful process of rebuilding, I discovered parts of myself I never knew existed. I found strength I didn't know I had. I reclaimed dreams I had set aside. I built a new vision for my life—one that was truly mine.

When facing flexibility challenges, the key questions to ask yourself are:

- What am I being asked to let go of, and what might be waiting on the other side?
- How can I remain open to new possibilities even amid grief?
- What parts of my identity remain solid even as circumstances change?
- Where can I find meaning in this transformation?

Flexibility training builds adaptability, openness, and resilience—qualities that help you navigate change with grace instead of resistance.

I had to lean so deeply into myself during that time of the triple threat storm. It's easy to know who you are when everyone affirms it. But can you hold onto that knowing when people and circumstances are actively trying to tear it down? That was the real test.

At the same time, my daughters were watching. How I handled adversity would shape how they handled theirs.

So let me ask you this: What if the adversity you're facing right now isn't meant to break you, but to reveal strength you didn't know you had? What if the storm isn't meant to destroy you, but to develop you?

YOUR PERSONAL STRENGTH TRAINING

I've learned to think of adversity like going to the gym. You don't walk into a workout expecting it to be comfortable— you go because you know the resistance will make you stronger. Life's challenges work the same way. They're not punishments; they're your personal training sessions, designed to build muscles you didn't even know you needed.

But just like at the gym, you need the right approach to get the most benefit from the workout.

Start by identifying what kind of training you're in. Not all adversities are the same. Some build endurance, some create resistance, and others force flexibility. When you can name what type you're facing, you can approach it with the right mindset:

Endurance challenges require pacing and sustainability. Ask yourself: "How can I break this down into manageable steps?"

Resistance challenges call for boundaries and standing firm. Ask yourself: "What truth do I need to hold onto regardless of opposition?"

Flexibility challenges demand adaptation and openness. Ask yourself: "What am I being asked to release, and what might I gain in return?"

Once you know your training type, look deeper. Every challenge targets something specific in you. Maybe your current adversity is developing your patience while waiting for test results. Perhaps it's building your discernment about which voices to listen to, or your courage to face uncomfortable truths. It might be strengthening your ability to advocate for yourself or teaching you to protect what matters most.

When you can name the specific strength being developed, suddenly there's purpose in the pain.

But here's the thing about strength training—you can't do it alone. No athlete trains without support, and neither should you. You need people in your corner, but not just anyone. Be intentional about building your team:

Your coaches—therapists, counselors, mentors—provide the guidance and expertise you need. Your teammates understand your specific struggle because they've been there too. Your cheerleaders remind you of your strength when you forget you have any. And your spiritual spotters pray for you and help carry the weight when it gets too heavy.

Not everyone deserves access to your journey. Choose your training partners wisely.

Finally, track your progress like any serious athlete would. Keep a journal of small victories. Notice how you're handling challenges differently than you would have before. Celebrate when old triggers don't affect you as strongly. Document moments of peace amid the difficulty.

This becomes evidence of your growth when doubt inevitably creeps in.

Now, with all this in mind, take a moment to assess where you are:

• What current challenge are you facing that feels overwhelming? How might it be building strength you'll need later?

• Think about your biggest past challenge. What muscles did it build that you're still using today?

• Where in your life are you resisting the very adversity that might be trying to strengthen you?

• Which type of strength training—endurance, resistance, or flexibility—is your current situation most like? How does understanding this change your approach?

• Who are your training partners for this season? Who might you need to add to your corner?

Strength isn't built in comfort. Wisdom isn't found in ease. Trust isn't developed on sunny days. Our adversities don't break us—they reveal us. They show us what we're truly made of, and more importantly, what we're capable of becoming.

It's not about whether adversity will come—it will. The question is whether we'll trust it enough to let it do its work in us.

PART THREE
REBUILDING TRUST

CHAPTER EIGHT

TRUSTING YOUR VOICE
WHEN VOICES COLLIDE

Sometimes the hardest voices to silence are the ones inside our own head—but not the voice that's truly ours. The hardest voices to silence are the ones we've internalized from others, the chorus of expectations and judgments that drown out our authentic inner knowing.

If you can relate, know that you're not alone. For years, I questioned my instincts, muted my true voice, doubted my perceptions. I deferred to the voices of others—some with good intentions, some not—until at times I wasn't sure if I could even hear my own voice anymore.

And one of the greatest lessons I've learned about distinguishing between these competing voices came through watching my daughter navigate the same battle.

Christine has taught me more about trusting my authentic inner voice than any book or therapist ever could.

Starting in her sophomore year of high school, Christine began dressing exactly as she wanted—dramatic makeup, gothic style, clothes that reflected her artistic soul. As her mom, I found myself getting anxious. Not because I didn't love who she was, but because I could hear all those external voices so clearly: *What will people think? She'll be judged. She's making herself a target.*

I'd watch people stare when we were out together, and those voices would get louder: *See? People are looking. This isn't safe. She should tone it down.*

When she went off to college in a conservative town, I held my breath. She'd come home with stories of the looks she got, the judgment she faced, and I could hear those external voices saying, *I told you so. This is exactly what you should be afraid of.*

What's embarrassing to admit is that it showed me my own blind spots. If someone else's child was expressing themselves boldly, my inner voice would say, "Good for you! Be yourself!" But when it was my own daughter, the external voices of fear and judgment towards her drowned out my authentic response.

But here's what changed everything: watching Christine consistently choose to listen to *her* inner voice over the external chorus of judgment.

She doesn't hate what she wears—she feels powerful in it. She doesn't apologize for her style—she owns it completely. What she hates isn't her authentic expression; what she hates is that people are judgmental. But even knowing that judgment exists, she refuses to let those external voices override her inner knowing of who she is.

When she transferred to a new city with a vibrant artistic community, everything shifted for her. Professors loved her. Bosses appreciated her creativity and work ethic. Adults were drawn to her authenticity and her heart. She found her people—those who could see past the surface to the incredible person underneath.

The truth is, there will always be voices telling us to be smaller, safer, more palatable. But our inner voice—the one that knows who we really are—deserves to be heard above all that noise.

Her willingness to trust her authentic inner knowing, regardless of external judgment, gave me permission I didn't know I needed. If my daughter could tune out the chorus of criticism and listen to her inner truth, what was stopping me from doing the same?

"You have every right to trust your inner voice about who you are," I found myself telling her during one particularly difficult moment. "Don't let external voices convince you to be anyone other than yourself."

The words flowed easily when I was talking to her. But why had it been so hard to apply that same wisdom to myself? Why did I so readily encourage her to trust her inner voice while letting external voices override my own?

One of the hardest parts about parenting is watching our children struggle with the same things we do. With Christine, it might have been the challenge of having her feelings dismissed or being labeled "too dramatic" for expressing herself authentically. With my other daughter Kate, it's been learning to trust her own desires even when they don't align with what's expected of her.

These aren't coincidences that they struggle with the things we struggle with as well. Our children inherit not just our DNA but our emotional patterns and our unresolved wounds. They watch how we navigate the world and, consciously or unconsciously, adopt similar strategies.

I think many of us reclaim our authentic voice this way

—through fiercely defending someone else's right to theirs. We become advocates for our children's inner knowing in ways we've never managed for ourselves.

And in doing so, we begin to hear our own authentic voice again—the one that's been there all along, waiting for us to trust it above all the external noise.

A close friend went through her divorce about seven months before mine, and taught me something life-changing about boundaries. Her husband was an alcoholic who would drive their children around while intoxicated—a situation she had endured for seven years while trying desperately to get him into treatment. "I finally had to set a boundary in my marriage and ultimately leave," she told me one afternoon, "because I was terrified my children would grow up thinking this was normal—that they should accommodate dangerous behavior."

She described how her children would come to her frustrated and scared because of their dad's actions. "What finally pushed me to leave wasn't even how he treated me," she confessed, tears in her eyes. "It was seeing the fear in my daughter's face and realizing that if I stayed, I was teaching her this was acceptable. Turns out, I deserved those boundaries too. But I couldn't see it until I saw it through her eyes."

The beautiful truth is that our children don't just inherit our wounds—they also inherit our capacity for healing. And they don't just witness our struggles—they watch us transform them into wisdom. They learn from our growth.

In trying to be strong for my kids, I discovered strength I never knew I had—partly because of Christine's encouragement. She began to tell me I deserved better. I was shocked. During my divorce, Christine even bought me a coffee mug that said "Enjoy the Adventure"—her way of encouraging me to see this painful transition as the beginning of something new rather than just an ending. That simple gesture showed me she understood that sometimes the scariest changes lead to the most beautiful chapters.

So in trying to model trusting my voice, I actually began to trust it. In trying to give them permission to speak their truth, I gave myself that same permission.

When I finally found the courage to leave a marriage that required my silence, I wasn't just changing my own life —I was showing my daughters what it looks like to value yourself enough to walk away from what diminishes you. When I rebuilt my life after divorce, cancer, and corporate betrayal, I wasn't just demonstrating resilience—I was teaching them that brokenness isn't the end of the story.

Both my daughters have referenced these experiences at different times, showing me how deeply they were paying attention to the choices I was making and the strength I was finding.

This is the quiet miracle of relationships: sometimes the healing we seek for others becomes our own.

LEARNING TO DISTINGUISH VOICES

Kate and I were talking about college applications recently. I'd told her she needed to apply to five schools, and after finishing four, she was stuck on the fifth choice. So I asked her, "If you could dream big, where would you really want to go?"

Without hesitation, she said, "St. John's in New York."

"Then apply," I told her. "Let's see what doors God opens."

As we talked more about New York, I could hear something in her voice—this sense of possibility, of doing something just for herself. And honestly? Her excitement stirred something in me too. I started thinking about all the versions of myself I'd never explored because I'd always chosen the safe path. Here was my daughter, ready to embrace possibility, and I found myself getting just as excited as she was.

Being a mom in these moments is tricky. You're constantly trying to figure out when to voice your fears and when to help them push past theirs. When to share your hard-earned wisdom and when to step back and let them earn their own.

In my head, all these voices start competing:

The practical mother: *"But what about the extra cost? What about the distance?"*

The healing mother: *"But what about her joy? Her growth? What if this is the path that brings her alive in ways you can't even imagine?"*

The fearful mother: *"But what if she struggles making friends easily and gets homesick? What if something happens and you can't get to her quickly?"*

The faithful mother: *"But what if God is opening this door for a reason?"*

What I've learned is that good mothering means recognizing all these voices will show up, but I get to choose which one gets the final say. And more and more, I'm trusting the voice that whispers, "Let her walk her own path, even when it's different from yours."

That night, I was journaling about our conversation when it hit me—I wasn't just learning to trust her voice. I was learning to trust my own again. The voice that says it's okay to want more, to follow what calls to you even when nobody else understands it, to trust that quiet knowing inside even when everyone else is telling you to play it safe.

Here's the thing: those voice collisions never go away. They show up in relationships, at work, in every decision that really matters. What other people expect will always compete with what you know deep down. The easy path will always try to pull you away from your truth.

But what if those moments aren't roadblocks? What if they're actually opportunities—not to pick one voice over another, but to find a way for them all to work together?

I'm realizing that trusting my voice doesn't mean I have to be the loudest person in the room. Sometimes it means getting quiet enough to actually hear the wisdom others are offering. Sometimes it means saying, "I don't know yet," and giving myself space to listen for that still, small voice that knows things my busy mind hasn't figured out yet.

And sometimes? It means admitting I got it wrong and starting over.

So how do you figure out which voice to trust when they're all talking at once? This is honestly the question I've wrestled with most in learning to trust myself again. Here's what I've discovered:

Your real voice feels different than the others.

Those critical voices are harsh and mean. They say things like "You might mess up," or "You'll never get this right." But your true voice? It's clear without being cruel. It might challenge you, but it doesn't beat you up.

I've learned to tell the difference by paying attention to how they make me feel. My authentic voice brings clarity—

sometimes even relief—even when it's telling me something hard. But that critical voice shaped by everyone else's expectations? It always leaves me feeling small and anxious.

Your authentic voice often speaks through your body.

Pay attention to physical sensations when making decisions. Tightness in your chest, a knot in your stomach—these are often your body's way of saying "This doesn't align with who you truly are."

When I was considering whether to leave my marriage, my body knew long before my mind could admit it. I'd get headaches before going home. I got a physical rash on my wedding ring finger under the ring. My shoulders would tense whenever I heard my husband's car in the driveway. My body was telling me what my conscious mind wasn't ready to hear: this relationship no longer felt safe.

Your authentic voice doesn't rush you.

Unlike anxiety, which demands immediate action to escape discomfort, your inner wisdom gives you space to reflect. It doesn't fade when you sit with it; it clarifies. This is why I journal so much, and why I sit in silence to do my devotionals.

True wisdom tends to be persistent but patient. It doesn't demand you act this instant; it simply remains steady, gently returning to your awareness until you're ready to listen.

Your authentic voice stays consistent.

External opinions might shift with trends or others' moods, but your inner knowing remains steady. The same whisper that says "This relationship isn't right" will still be there weeks later, even if you try to ignore it.

What's fascinating is how my intuition about my marriage stayed consistent for years, despite my attempts to silence it. The concerns I journaled about in 2003 were the same ones that ultimately led to our separation in 2020. My authentic voice had been trying to get my attention for decades.

Your authentic voice often sounds like the you before you learned to doubt yourself.

Think of how children speak before they learn to filter— direct, honest, clear about their needs and boundaries. That clarity is still within you.

I see this in my daughters all the time. Before the world teaches them to second-guess themselves, they have this beautiful certainty about what they want and need. "I don't like that," my older daughter would say as a child, without a hint of apology. That directness is clarity we've forgotten how to access.

I've learned to distinguish my true voice by asking specific questions:

Does this voice bring me closer to or further from peace? Trust tends to create an inner settling, even when the message is challenging.

Would I speak to someone I love the way this voice

speaks to me? If you wouldn't say it to your daughter or best friend, it's probably not your authentic voice.

Does this voice expand possibilities or limit them? Your true voice opens doors; the critical voice builds walls.

Is this voice mine, or am I echoing someone else's expectations? Sometimes we internalize others' voices so completely we mistake them for our own.

Five years from now, will I regret listening to or ignoring this voice? This question helps cut through immediate fears to connect with deeper wisdom.

These questions have become a compass when voices collide within me. They help me find my way back to myself, even when the path isn't clear.

I've been changed by watching my daughters claim their right to their feelings, their boundaries, their dreams. When I see Christine being her true, unapologetic authentic self, or hear Kate articulate desires that have nothing to do with pleasing others, I'm witnessing courage that inspires my own. When they stand in their truth even when it's uncomfortable, they're showing me what authenticity looks like in action.

Sometimes the truest voice in the room belongs to someone who refuses to silence themselves to keep peace, who stands in their truth even when it's inconvenient, who chooses authenticity over accommodation. And in those moments, our job isn't to guide their path but to stand in awe of their courage and to learn from it.

COMING HOME TO YOUR VOICE

The journey to trusting your voice is really about coming home to yourself. It's about learning to distinguish between the voice of fear that says, "Stay quiet," and the voice of truth that says, "Speak up." It's about understanding that your voice matters—not because it's perfect, but because it's authentically yours.

Sometimes trusting your voice means standing alone. Sometimes it means being labeled "difficult." Sometimes it means walking away from relationships that require you to silence yourself. But what I've learned—what I watch my daughters learning—is that the price of silencing your voice is always higher than the cost of speaking it.

Take some time to reflect on your own relationship with your voice:

• When was the last time you silenced your voice to keep peace? What was the cost?

• What voices—internal or external—most often cause you to doubt yourself?

• Think of a time you trusted your voice despite opposition. What gave you the courage?

• Where in your life right now are you choosing silence over truth?

• What would change if you fully trusted your voice?

Here's what I want you to hear today: Your voice isn't too much. It's not too strong, too emotional, too anything. It's simply yours. And that makes it worth trusting.

In the end, trusting your voice isn't about drowning out others—it's about learning to hear your own above the noise. It's about realizing that in a world full of competing voices, the one most worth listening to is often the quietest one—the one that speaks from your deepest truth.

CHAPTER NINE

TRUSTING YOUR INNER
TRUTH-TELLER

PEACE ISN'T JUST A FEELING—IT'S A TRUTH-TELLER.

I used to search for peace in all the wrong places. Achievement, being the perfect wife and mother, making everyone around me happy. I chased it through pharmaceutical sales, down fashion runways, into the corners of what looked like a perfect life. But real peace? It's not found in doing more—it's found in being aligned with who you really are.

The wake-up call came in 2014 when I hired what I thought was a business coach. On her intake form, the first question was simple: "What do you want more of?" Without thinking, I wrote one word: "Peace."

That surprised me. I had everything that should bring peace—successful career, seemingly stable marriage, healthy kids. All the external markers of a life well-lived. But underneath it all was this constant unrest, this nagging feeling that something wasn't quite right.

Peace isn't a destination you arrive at—it's an internal

navigation system trying to guide you home to yourself. And I'd been ignoring mine for years.

This inner guidance system isn't something you need to create—it already exists within you. It's been collecting data your entire life, making connections between experiences, emotions, and outcomes that your conscious mind might not even register. That's why you can sometimes feel unsettled about a situation before you can articulate why it's problematic.

Learning to trust this inner wisdom doesn't mean ignoring logic or practical considerations. It means including your intuitive knowing as a valid and valuable source of information alongside other factors. In fact, the deepest wisdom often emerges when our rational understanding aligns with our intuitive sense—when our head and heart reach the same conclusion.

I learned to pay attention to this the hard way.

In 2011, my husband and I were feeling unsettled in the town where I grew up. We had moved there after Steve finished law school because we wanted to start a family near our support system. But years later, we found ourselves questioning: Is this it? Is this all there is? Have I just defaulted to the familiar rather than creating a life that truly feels like me?

After many conversations, we decided to make a bold move to Austin—a city we loved for its outdoorsy lifestyle, music festivals, and vibrant culture. We took a leap of faith, packed up our family, bought a house, and prepared to restart our businesses.

On paper, it should have been exciting. In reality, my peace meter immediately went into the red zone.

While my income would continue from my existing

business, I needed to travel back and forth to maintain it while simultaneously building in our new location. Meanwhile, our daughters were just four and eight years old, and I was determined to help them establish new friendships—but only with families I personally vetted, which required enormous time and energy. I found myself stretched impossibly thin—trying to be a present mother, maintain our primary income, and establish an entirely new life.

The physical toll was unmistakable. I was exhausted, stressed, and depleting myself daily. We had purchased a home that stretched our finances further than was comfortable. Our marriage began deteriorating as I witnessed choices that contradicted what I valued. Everything cost more than we anticipated. My oldest daughter started struggling in school. What had seemed like an adventure had become an endless uphill battle where nothing—absolutely nothing—came easily.

About eighteen months in, we finally acknowledged the truth my peace meter had been signaling from the beginning: this wasn't right for us. Of course, admitting defeat felt like failure. "What will people think of us?" we worried. "Have we failed?" But ultimately, we decided we were proud for having tried something bold, even if it hadn't worked out. We made the decision to return to the familiar, where we had support and established income streams.

Looking back, I can see how this experience, challenging as it was, still served a greater purpose. Moving to Austin actually expanded my business in unexpected ways, ultimately increasing my income and growing my team. But when the peace inside me was so significantly disrupted—when every day felt like swimming against a powerful current—it wasn't just stress or adjustment. It was my intuition speaking clearly through my body, telling me this path wasn't aligned with my authentic self.

Now when I face decisions, I pay careful attention to my peace meter. Does this choice bring deep exhalation or constriction? Does it create space or pressure? The Austin experiment taught me that peace isn't just a nice-to-have feeling—it's essential information about whether I'm moving toward or away from my authentic path.

The real breakthrough came when I started treating peace as a non-negotiable rather than a nice-to-have. Instead of pushing through situations that disturbed my peace, I began to pause and ask why. This didn't mean running away from every uncomfortable situation—growth often requires discomfort. But there's a difference between the discomfort of growth and the discomfort of being out of alignment with your truth.

When I finally filed for divorce from Steve, it wasn't peaceful in the conventional sense—it was the hardest thing I've ever done. I had just dropped my oldest daughter off at college, helping her move into her dorm on a Sunday. The next day, after seeing her settling into her new life, I drove the seven longest hours of my life back home. Walking up the stairs to where my husband was living separately in our garage apartment, I said the words that would change everything: "I want a divorce."

The decision wasn't peaceful in terms of external circumstances, but underneath the pain and fear was a different kind of peace—the peace that comes from finally aligning with your truth, even when that truth is difficult. It wasn't about the absence of conflict; it was about the presence of alignment with my authentic self. I could exhale freely for the first time in years.

When I'm working with my sales team now, I can feel physically when something isn't aligned with my values. Last year, I was considering an additional business opportunity that looked perfect on paper—great financial incentives, solid reputation, expanded market reach. But every time I thought about the opportunity or reviewed the details, my body would send clear signals: my shoulders would tense, my breathing would become shallow, and I'd feel unsettled, almost sick to my stomach. My peace meter was giving me a clear reading.

Despite the apparent advantages and external pressure to move forward, it took me months—nearly a year—to fully acknowledge what my body already knew. This opportunity, promising as it seemed, would compromise the values I hold most dear: the flexibility to be my true authentic self, the ability to live life on my terms, and the freedom to be fully present for my new blended family. My internal truth-teller recognized this misalignment long before my logical mind was ready to admit it.

I trusted that internal signal and declined the opportunity. After saying no to that opportunity, I felt super at ease —like I could finally take a full breath again. What happened next confirmed I'd made the right choice. Over the next year, my business grew in ways that wouldn't have been possible if I'd added in something else. Even more importantly, the time I was able to invest in blending our family created results that were absolutely exponential. Watching my girls and my husband (more about him soon!) Beau's boys form real connections, seeing our new family take shape—that was the real prize. My gut wasn't just telling me what wasn't right for me; it was making space for something so much better.

As we talked about in the last chapter, sometimes our intuition speaks most clearly through our children. When my daughter Christine was at college in Lubbock, I remember having this feeling from the beginning that it wasn't the right fit for her. She was so artistic, and Lubbock is... well, it's pretty remote. But she'd been dead set on going there, so I supported her decision.

After two years, she came to me one day and said, "Mom, I haven't shared this with you, but I'm miserable here. I cannot come back. I do not want to be here. I've felt this way all year." She'd even prepared this whole presentation about transferring schools.

I had been noticing external signs for a while but partially ignoring them—the way we often do when we're trying to prove to ourselves that we're on the right path. There's that internal debate: should I continue on this path I've committed to, or am I receiving signs that things aren't aligning? With Christine's situation, my intuition was clearly nudging me: this is your chance to listen to what you've been feeling all along, to acknowledge the signs instead of rationalizing them away.

I told Christine, "Look, we're going to go through this process just like I think the Lord wants us to. We'll let Him open and close doors." We started with practical steps— meeting with an admissions advisor at the University of North Texas to see what credits would transfer. She didn't want to lose credits or have to stay in school longer, which made sense.

Then we looked at what her major would look like at UNT, how to get out of her lease in Lubbock, how her roommates would find someone to replace her—all those practical details that can make a big decision feel overwhelming.

But through the whole process, my gut kept telling me: "You've got to walk through this door with her." And I'm so glad I listened. She ended up transferring schools, and she could not be happier. It's been the best choice for her.

Our intuition isn't some mystical sixth sense—it's our brain processing information so quickly that we feel the conclusion before we can articulate why. That feeling of unease is actually our mind connecting dots our conscious brain hasn't caught up with yet.

Yet we often dismiss our intuition because we can't explain it logically. We've been taught to need "proof" before we trust our gut. But think about it—our ancestors who survived long enough to become our ancestors were the ones who listened when something felt off, who ran when they sensed danger before they could name it.

When you're not at peace, don't just try to push through or explain it away. Listen to what that discomfort is trying to tell you. Because sometimes that unease is the most loving guidance you'll ever receive—your internal compass pointing you back toward your authentic path.

READING YOUR OWN INNER TRUTH-TELLER

Different people experience their inner truth-teller in different ways. For me it may be peace, but for some, it's a gut instinct—an undeniable pull that either draws them toward something or warns them to step away. Others experience it as a quiet knowing, a persistent thought that won't let go. Some people feel it physically—a tightness in the chest, a headache, exhaustion that sets in when they're veering off course.

For me, when I'm aligned, I feel it as a deep exhale, a

sense of certainty even in the midst of uncertainty. And when I'm not? My body tenses, my mind races, and I start trying to logic my way out of what my spirit already knows.

Another big clue I've noticed—when I'm at peace with something, it stops consuming my mind. I can go about my day, focus on my family, be present in work conversations. But when I'm out of alignment? Oh my goodness, it's like that thing takes up permanent residence in my head! I'll be driving, making dinner, or trying to fall asleep, and there it is again. That relationship. That decision. That opportunity. My mind keeps circling back to it over and over, like it's waving a giant red flag saying, "Hey! Pay attention to this!"

Our intuition is at its loudest in matters of safety, and this isn't just about physical danger. It's about emotional safety too. When someone makes you feel anxious, when a situation causes you to constantly second-guess yourself, when a relationship has you walking on eggshells—that's your built-in warning system going off.

I've come to think of intuition as God's GPS system—it's that still, small voice that guides us if we'll only listen. We're fearfully and wonderfully made, with internal guidance systems designed to help us navigate life. But like any GPS, it only works if you turn it on and actually follow the directions.

Beau had been with UPS for years in a position he enjoyed, working for a boss he deeply respected and trusted. Then an opportunity arose in a different division—Global Business Systems—that his mentor was strongly encouraging him to pursue.

On paper, it looked like advancement. Better title, new challenges, potential for growth. But the situation wasn't straightforward. His current boss, someone whose judgment Beau valued tremendously, was actually discouraging him from making the change.

"I'm so torn," Beau told me one evening as we sat on our back porch. "I love my current boss. I trust him. He's been right about so many things in the past."

But something felt off. Despite his respect for his boss's opinion, Beau couldn't shake this persistent feeling that he needed to make the move. It wasn't logical—it was purely intuitive. That quiet, nagging sensation that sometimes there's more information available to our spirit than to our conscious mind.

After weeks of deliberation, Beau decided to follow his gut rather than the advice of his trusted boss. It felt uncomfortable and a bit disloyal, but that inner compass kept pointing firmly toward change.

Just a few months after he made the transition to the new division, his old department announced significant layoffs. Had he stayed, he would have lost his position. That inner knowing—that inexplicable unease that pushed him toward a different path—had protected him from a future he couldn't have logically predicted.

So sometimes our inner truth-teller speaks to us through discomfort rather than peace. Sometimes that unsettled feeling isn't anxiety to push through—it's wisdom trying to protect us.

Looking back on experiences like these builds our trust muscles. When we recognize how our intuition has guided us correctly in the past—even when it didn't make rational sense at the time—we become more willing to listen to it in the future. We start collecting evidence of our own inner wisdom, proving to ourselves that we can trust that quiet voice within.

That's why it's so important to acknowledge these moments even after the fact. Each time we recognize how our inner guidance system steered us right, we're building a stronger case for trusting ourselves next time. We're collecting proof that our prayers are being answered, that our internal compass knows the way even when our logical mind can't see the whole picture.

This trust muscle, like any other, gets stronger with use. The more we listen to and honor our intuition, the more clearly it speaks to us—and the more confident we become in following it, even when the path it points to seems uncertain.

Learning to recognize your personal truth-teller requires paying attention to how your body, mind, and emotions respond in different situations. It requires stepping back from the noise of the world and tuning in to your own signals.

Here are some practical ways to develop your peace meter:

1. Start a Peace Journal

Begin documenting situations where you feel at peace versus those where you feel unsettled. Look for patterns. What kinds of decisions, environments, or relationships consistently disturb your peace? Which ones enhance it?

Pay special attention to the physical sensations that accompany both states. Where do you feel tension when you're out of alignment? Where do you feel expansion when something is right?

2. Practice the Pause

When facing a decision, big or small, create space between the question and your answer. Take a deep breath.

Check in with your body. Notice what happens inside when you consider different options.

This pause interrupts our habitual responses and creates room for our intuition to speak. It's in this space that we often hear the wisdom that our busy minds might otherwise miss.

3. Do Regular Peace Checks

Throughout your day, pause and ask yourself: "Am I at peace right now? If not, why?"

Sometimes the answer will be obvious—you're stuck in traffic or running late for a meeting. But other times, you might discover a deeper misalignment that needs attention —perhaps you're in a conversation that feels inauthentic, or you've agreed to something that doesn't honor your boundaries.

4. Look for External Confirmations

While your internal peace meter is your primary guide, external signs often confirm its readings. Doors that myste-riously open or close, comments from trusted friends that resonate deeply, recurring themes or messages—all of these can be confirmations of what your intuition is already telling you.

In Beau's story with the job change that protected him from layoffs, the external confirmation strengthened his trust in his intuition for future decisions.

5. Create a Peace Meter Evidence List

Like the resilience inventory we discussed earlier, create a list of times when your peace meter guided you correctly. These might be situations where:

- You ignored a warning feeling and later regretted it
- You trusted your gut against logic and it proved right

• You felt drawn to something without understanding why, and it led to something important

• You experienced deep peace about a decision that others questioned

This evidence list becomes a powerful reminder that your inner guidance system works, that it's trustworthy, and that it deserves your attention.

Consider these questions to help you identify your inner truth-teller:

• When was the last time you felt a strong gut reaction about something? What did it tell you, and were you right to trust it?

• Have you ever ignored a persistent thought or feeling, only to later realize it was trying to guide you?

• How does your body react when something isn't right?

• What situations make you feel most energized, clear, and confident?

The key to trusting your inner truth-teller is first identifying how it speaks to you. Sometimes, it's subtle—a flicker of doubt, an unshakable curiosity, a hesitation that you can't quite explain. Sometimes it just says "no," without explanation, without reasons. And that's okay. You don't need to justify your intuition to anyone, not even yourself.

I can't think of a single time I regretted listening to my intuition. But I can think of plenty of times I regretted ignoring it. That alone tells me everything I need to know about whose voice I should be trusting.

Your inner truth-teller isn't just valuable in avoiding danger or making major life decisions. It's also your guide to a life of alignment, where your outer circumstances match your inner values. When you learn to trust this voice—to hear it above the noise of shoulds and expectations—you discover a kind of peace that no external success can provide.

This is the peace that passes understanding—not because it defies logic, but because it goes deeper than logic. It's the peace that comes from walking in truth, from honoring the wisdom God planted within you, from trusting that your inner knowing is a gift, not a distraction to be overcome.

So the next time your peace meter sends you a signal, remember: it's not trying to derail you. It's trying to guide you home to yourself.

CHAPTER TEN

TRUSTING YOURSELF TO START AGAIN

WHEN I GOT MY FIRST TATTOO—ISAIAH 41:10 DOWN MY SPINE— it was a declaration of freedom from old constraints. Your spine holds you up, and for me, that verse has been my backbone through cancer and divorce: "Fear not, for I am with you" (NKJV). Getting it tattooed felt like honoring a part of me I had learned to quiet over the years—more out of love and respect for others than from my own conviction.

In the journey to start building a life that aligned with who I am, one of the most important moments was finding my rental home. I knew I had to get to a safe place—somewhere away from the chaos and pain, somewhere I could begin healing and learning to trust myself again.

When I found this little house, I couldn't believe the street name: Liberty Lane. I mean, could there be a more perfect symbol? I was seeking freedom, peace, and a fresh start, and here was this home quite literally on the path to liberty.

I used to call it my "sanctuary." I made it so girly and

peaceful—just what I needed at that time and what I hoped my girls needed too. I was proud to have people come over, proud of myself for finding it and making it my own. It was the first time in so long that I'd created a space that was truly mine, that reflected who I was becoming rather than who I'd been.

Initially, I was determined to buy something. I had this idea that I needed to immediately replace the home I'd left with another permanent one. But God had other plans, and He brought me such peace when I finally decided that maybe renting made more sense. My brother-in-law was actually the one who convinced me of that.

The way it all came together still amazes me. I made one phone call to a friend who I knew had rented due to a flood in her house. She said, "Yeah, I moved out just three weeks ago. That house is available. Why don't you call the landlord?"

When she mentioned his name, I nearly dropped the phone. "Wait—the guy who owns the daycare my kids went to? The one whose mom owned the daycare I went to when I was little?" I couldn't believe it. This wasn't just any land-lord; this was someone connected to my life, someone I already trusted.

He met me that same day. The house was perfect and affordable. He promised to take care of me, said there was no strict contract, and I could stay as long as I needed. Some furniture would even be left behind to help me get started. Everything just aligned so beautifully.

That house on Liberty Lane became my first step in rebuilding my life. It was confirmation that I was on the right path. As I arranged my belongings and decorated the rooms, each decision was mine alone to make. What color throw pillows did *I* want? Which pictures brought *me* joy? For the first time in decades, I wasn't compromising my taste or seeking approval for my choices.

Sometimes starting over doesn't mean immediately jumping into another permanent situation—sometimes it means giving yourself the grace of a temporary sanctuary while you figure out who you're becoming. Creating this space taught me to trust my own instincts about what I needed to feel safe, comfortable, and authentic.

Starting over after divorce brings the pillar of Trusting Your Decisions into sharp focus. Suddenly, you're faced with decisions large and small—where to live, how to parent alone, whether to date, how to structure your finances— without the partner you've relied on for decades. These decisions can feel overwhelming, especially when your confidence has been shattered.

Decision-making is a muscle that grows stronger with use. Each time I made a choice that honored my authentic needs—from the throw pillows to the boundary-setting—I was rebuilding my trust in my own judgment. Each time a decision turned out well, it became evidence that I could trust myself again.

The next challenge was navigating the modern dating world. Dating apps? Coffee meets? The landscape had changed dramatically since I last dated in my early twenties. I remember sitting with my phone, trying to decide what to write in my profile on a dating app, what photos to use, how to present myself authentically while still protecting my heart.

Who am I now? What do I even want in a relationship? Am I

ready for this? These questions swirled through my mind as I stared at the blank profile screen.

At first, I felt nauseous so I had to stop and put it away for several weeks. That compass was telling me "not yet"—until then it became time. I noticed the difference between fear (which I could push through) and that genuine internal caution that said, "You need more time." Learning to distinguish between these feelings was crucial to rebuilding trust in starting again.

One of the first lessons I learned was to bring a twenty-dollar bill on first dates. It might sound trivial, but having the ability to exit quickly if needed gave me a sense of control I desperately needed. After one particularly uncomfortable date where I had to wait to sign a credit card bill while wanting to leave, I learned the value of having an escape plan!

Never again will I be stuck in a situation where I can't follow my instincts, I promised myself.

But the challenge was bigger than learning the mechanics of dating—it was learning to trust my instincts again. After years of questioning my own reality and carrying the weight of self-doubt in my marriage, how could I trust my judgment about men? How could I tell the difference between legitimate red flags and my own fears of just screwing up?

The answer came through an unexpected source—my business coaching work. I started approaching dating the same way I approached training women in business: as an opportunity for growth and learning. Every date, whether it went well or poorly, became a chance to learn something—about myself, about what I wanted, about what I wouldn't tolerate.

And the lessons were frequent.

I remember during New Year's Day one year I had this whole day to myself—just me, on my own time. There was something so liberating about that.

I'd been trying to embrace this new season of my life. Going out alone, having a glass of wine at a restaurant by myself—these small acts of independence had become really important to me. They were helping me rediscover who I was outside of my marriage.

So there I was, sitting at this Italian restaurant in the mall, just enjoying a glass of wine after returning a Christmas gift. I checked the dating app I'd reluctantly put myself on, and this guy had messaged me. When I mentioned I was out in Dallas, he suggested meeting right then.

I decided to say yes. Part of starting over is being open to new experiences, right? *What's the worst that could happen?* I thought. *I'm in a public place, I've already had a nice day—why not take a chance?* I was trying to trust that I could handle whatever came my way.

When he arrived at the restaurant, my intuition immediately flashed a warning. The first thing he said was that he only dated women who were 5'11" or taller. Right away, I felt like a checkbox rather than a person. Next, he was immediately too familiar, too touchy for someone I'd just met.

Something doesn't feel right, my inner voice whispered. The hairs on the back of my neck stood up slightly. It wasn't fear exactly—more like a gentle warning system activating.

I tried to engage in normal conversation—asking about his life, his work, his background. But every time I'd ask something about his past, he'd shut it down. "Let's not talk about our past. Let's focus on right now."

That discomfort in my gut was growing stronger, but I second-guessed myself. *Maybe I'm overreacting. Maybe this is just how dating works now. Maybe I'm being too personal too soon.*

These thoughts felt eerily familiar. This is exactly where I went wrong in my marriage for years—ignoring that inner voice that was trying to protect me.

When I finally called him out for gaslighting me, his whole demeanor changed. He cursed at me and started ranting about his traumatic past. At that moment, I knew I needed to leave immediately. *Trust yourself. Trust yourself. Trust yourself.* The phrase repeated in my mind as I grabbed my purse, walked straight out to my car, locked the doors, and blocked his number.

That terrible date became a turning point. Each time I honored my internal alarms instead of dismissing them, I built back a little more self-trust. Each time I refused to accept poor treatment, I grew stronger in my conviction that I deserved better.

TO NEW BEGINNINGS

Starting over, I realized, isn't about erasing the past. It's about allowing the past to inform the future without defining it. It's understanding that the painful experiences, the betrayals, and the disappointments weren't just crises. They were lessons. Invitations to learn, to grow, to reclaim the inner wisdom I had spent too long ignoring.

As I reflected on my journey, I saw how each piece—the good, the bad, the beautiful, the brutal—had a role in shaping the woman I was becoming. A woman who was learning to trust herself again, one brave boundary at a time.

A woman who was giving herself permission to begin again, on her own terms.

So let me ask you this:

- What areas of your life are asking you to begin again? What fears are holding you back from taking those first steps?

- How have past disappointments or betrayals affected your ability to trust—not just others, but yourself?

- What would giving yourself "permission to begin again" look like in your current situation?

- How might your past experiences, even the painful ones, actually be preparing you for a new chapter?

Starting over is about willingness. The willingness to trust ourselves, our intuition, our hard-earned wisdom. The willingness to leave behind what doesn't serve us and reach for what does, even when it's terrifying. The willingness to rewrite our stories, not by erasing the past, but by allowing it to fuel a wiser future.

New beginnings, I've learned, aren't bestowed from the outside. They're cultivated from within. They begin the moment we look at our reflection—scars, mistakes, painful lessons and all—and decide that we're worthy of our own trust. The moment we say to ourselves, "I know you've been through a lot. I know you're scared. But I also know this: You can do hard things. You can start over. And I'll be with you, every shaky step of the way."

Permission to begin again doesn't come from anyone else. It comes from you. And you, dear one? You're so much stronger than you know. So let yourself begin. Trust the journey. And know that with each brave beginning, you're becoming more yourself.

CHAPTER ELEVEN

TRUSTING THE JOURNEY OF NEW BEGINNINGS

DATING AFTER DIVORCE AT FORTY-EIGHT WASN'T PART OF MY LIFE plan.

What I realized through all this was that I needed to let my dating path be led by the Lord because honestly, I had no idea what was best for me going forward. No clue at all.

I just decided to let the Lord open doors, and I'd walk through them. I remember friends who had all these rigid rules—they wouldn't date anyone who lived more than twenty miles away, or who had certain jobs, or whatever their criteria were. I threw all that out the window. I expanded my dating age range because, what did I know? What I thought I needed and what was actually best for me could be two completely different things.

When you've been through breaches of trust in such a significant relationship, everyone has an opinion about how you should heal. But at some point, you have to reclaim that authority over your own life. You have to trust that you— with God's guidance—know what's best for your heart, even when it defies conventional wisdom.

Then I met Beau. From our first exchanges on the dating app, I was drawn to his kindness and genuine communication style. He was responsive, thoughtful, and refreshingly absent of the games others played. There was an authenticity about him that felt like a breath of fresh air.

Of course, on paper, there were obstacles. He was nine years younger than me, covered in tattoos, and still technically married though separated for two years. He had three young boys. Was I ready to navigate a relationship with someone in such a different life stage? Initially, I thought, "Heck no!"—starting over with young children wasn't part of my plan.

But something kept drawing me back to this man.

My family was quietly cautious, their love for me wrapped in protection. My sisters showed gentle concern, and my brothers-in-law kept a watchful eye. They didn't have to say much—I could sense their hesitation, rooted in care and a deep desire to see me whole and happy.

But beneath all these external considerations was a quiet recognition—something in me saw something in Beau that transcended the obvious differences. There was a kindness in him, a genuine goodness that resonated with what I needed, not just what I thought I wanted.

The decision to trust that recognition wasn't easy. I mean, I broke up with him twice out of fear—that instinct to flee when things get real, when vulnerability feels too risky. But each time, I found myself drawn back by something stronger than fear: peace. Not the kind of peace that means everything is perfect, but the deep-seated knowledge that this was right, even when it was scary.

But again, I found I was stressing over what I was hearing from others: "It's too soon." "You need to heal first."

"You're almost an empty nester." I heard it from friends, from family members—these voices of concern that made me question my own judgment.

Should I listen to them? I wondered. *They love me and want what's best for me. But they haven't walked in my shoes. They don't feel what I'm feeling when I'm with him.* I was caught between what others thought was right and what felt right to me.

I actually had to talk to my trauma counselor about it. I wanted to know if there was a "right way" to do this—a proper timeline, a correct process, some formula that would guarantee I wouldn't get hurt again.

But what I discovered was the truth that's played out in every major challenge I've faced: there is no one way. There is no single correct path forward. There is no singular "right" formula.

When I was diagnosed with breast cancer, I remember sitting in the surgeon's office at that first appointment, and she started explaining my type of cancer. Then she said, "Here are the different ways we can handle it."

I was genuinely shocked. "What? No, just tell me what to do," I responded. "I don't want to have to make that decision. Why are there many decisions? Isn't there just one right way?"

Life rarely offers us a single correct solution. There are options, paths, possibilities—and they can all be valid. What works for one person might not work for another.

For my journey after divorce, healing didn't happen in isolation. It happened in the messiness of living, in the vulnerability of trying again, in the courage of opening my heart even while it was still tender. I found a person to heal with, and that became my story.

Not everyone's story, but mine.

And there's freedom in that, isn't there? Freedom in knowing we don't have to follow someone else's timeline or process. Freedom in trusting that God works uniquely in each of our lives. Freedom in knowing that your healing journey doesn't have to look like anyone else's to be valid.

I had to learn to quiet those external voices and listen more intently to that still, small voice within—the one that knew what I needed, even when others didn't understand it. The one that could sense when a door was opening, even when others thought it should stay closed.

I had always tried to be so responsible, always feeling like I had to run my decisions through someone else's filter —my parents, my ex-husband, my children. Part of what attracted me to Beau was the freedom to just be myself, to answer only to me. After decades of people-pleasing and fitting into others' expectations, I was finally giving myself permission to follow my own heart.

And it felt like God kept bringing me and Beau together in unexpected ways.

WHEN COINCIDENCES BECOME CONFIRMATIONS

Beau had been living in his marital home, and he needed a new place to live. He mentioned he'd be looking for a rental while figuring out his next steps.

"Yeah, I'm finally wrapping my head around selling it," he told me one day. "I'm gonna look for a place to rent because I don't know where I want to be next."

Literally the next day, I was walking down my stairwell

and glanced out my big picture window. There was a "For Rent" sign right across the street from my house.

I texted him as a total joke. I never thought in a million years he'd seriously consider moving in across from me. I mean, he lived about twenty minutes away in a completely different school district. We were just dating. But something made me send that text.

"Hey, guess what? There's a rental available right across from my house."

What started as a joke turned into a conversation, which turned into him actually considering it. One thing led to another, and suddenly it felt like more than coincidence. Little signs kept appearing, nudging us forward.

When Beau called about the rental, the timing wasn't quite right. His house had not even been put on the market yet, so he wasn't ready to move yet. In any normal rental market, especially in our area where properties move quickly, you'd expect the landlady to say, "Sorry, I need someone now. I can't hold it for you."

But that's not what happened.

Instead, she told him she'd wait. No deposit. No formal agreement. Just a simple, "I'll hold it until you're ready."

Who does that? In the Dallas rental market? Nobody.

When Beau told me this, I remember thinking, "That doesn't make financial sense for her." She could have easily found someone else willing to move in immediately. Why would she willingly leave the property vacant, losing income, just to wait for a stranger she'd only met briefly once?

The practical side of me—the side that's been responsible with money my entire life—couldn't make sense of it. But the faithful side of me? That part recognized it immediately as God's hand moving in ways I couldn't orchestrate myself.

It wasn't just that the house became available when Beau needed it. It wasn't just that it happened to be directly across from my house. It was that every potential obstacle kept falling away—including this landlady who, for reasons we couldn't understand, was willing to wait for him.

Beau and I both could see the writing on the wall.

"I don't understand why she's willing to do this," he told me. "But I'm not going to question it."

Later, after Beau had moved in and we got to know the landlady better, we discovered she was a woman of strong faith herself. I don't think she consciously held the property because of some spiritual prompting, but I do believe God works through people—sometimes without them even realizing they're being used as instruments.

That property being held for Beau without logical explanation became one of the clearest signals to me that this relationship was different—that it wasn't just my desires driving things forward, but something bigger than both of us creating a path.

I remember sitting with Beau and having serious conversations about what this would mean. "If we break up and you live across the street, how awkward is that going to be?" I worried. "What if the kids get attached and then things don't work out?"

Beau and I talked through all the what-ifs and how we would handle each scenario. But despite all the logical reasons to be cautious, there was this peace I felt—this sense that the doors were opening for a reason.

Living across the street from each other gave us a unique opportunity to build trust gradually. It allowed his boys to get to know me in a natural way. It allowed my daughters to get comfortable with the idea of this new person in our lives without the pressure of immediate cohabitation. It gave us time to learn each other's rhythms, to see each other in real life, not just dating life. It created this unique space where our relationship could grow stronger before we made bigger commitments.

Expanding Trust

One of the things that made our relationship work is how Beau's experience with his own divorce gave him a unique perspective on trust and healing. He understands trauma. Beau owns where he was at fault, and did from the very beginning. Even after his wife's betrayal, he took his ownership where he felt necessary. That emotional maturity was so attractive. He had done the hard work in counseling.

On our 3rd date, I explained how I had not forgiven the betrayal I experienced, and he so calmly told me how to in encouragement. He talked about how it would heal my heart in a way that would lead to peace. I was so touched, and this was the first time I recognized this man would be part of my healing journey.

One of the biggest differences in this relationship is how we handle emotional regulation. Beau comes from a family where emotions are expressed openly, where vulnerability is valued. His father is incredibly loving and emotionally available—a stark contrast to my own upbringing. Through him, I'm learning that being emotional isn't being "too much"—it's being authentically human.

Still, old patterns don't disappear overnight. There are moments when I become emotionally unregulated, when past trauma surfaces and I retreat into protective mode. I call it "abort mission" mode—where I suddenly feel like I can take care of myself, I don't need anyone, I should hibernate and isolate.

But instead of these moments threatening the relationship, they become opportunities for deeper connection. Beau understands that my need to isolate sometimes isn't about him—it's about me processing and regulating. He gives me space while letting me know I'm not alone.

Our different backgrounds—my conservative upbringing versus his more expressive, artistic nature—might seem like a potential source of conflict. Instead, they've become our strength. He helps me embrace parts of myself I'd learned to suppress.

Recently, we had a misunderstanding that triggered old insecurities. In my past, such moments would have led to withdrawal, to walls being built higher. But with Beau, even when emotions run high, there's a foundation of safety that allows us to work through the hard moments together because he wants to discuss it and not let anything go unsaid. The only way forward is communication, listening, and true understanding.

One of my deepest fears after my divorce was whether I could trust someone to truly care for me. Not just in grand romantic gestures, but in the everyday moments when I needed support. For years, I hadn't had my needs considered or prioritized, and that leaves a mark on your heart.

Early in our relationship, I would occasionally voice this fear to Beau. "Will you take care of me?" I'd ask, almost embarrassed by my vulnerability but unable to keep the question inside. The words felt small coming out of my mouth, but they represented mountains of past disappointment.

Then something happened that I never would have wished for, but that became one of the clearest signs God was guiding me toward trust again.

During a trip to New York, I broke my ankle. What should have been a simple weekend getaway turned into a painful ordeal that left me completely dependent on others once we returned home. I couldn't carry a glass of water across the kitchen because I was on crutches. I couldn't transport my computer. I couldn't navigate the stairs in my house.

That's when the blessing of Beau living across the street became abundantly clear.

Without hesitation, he stepped in to care for me completely. He made my meals, ensuring I ate properly. When his boys were with him, he'd feed them dinner, then come over with food for me, check what I needed, and return after putting them to bed to make sure I was comfortable for the night.

I remember sitting at my desk one afternoon, leg propped up, feeling frustrated by my limitations. I looked up to see Beau walking through my house carrying a basket of my laundry.

"What are you doing?" I asked, genuinely confused.

"I'm going to do your laundry," he said simply, as if it were the most natural thing in the world.

"I've never had a man do my laundry before," I told him, tears welling in my eyes.

It wasn't just about the laundry. It was about being cared for in practical, unglamorous ways—the kind of care that comes from genuine love rather than obligation. At that moment, I heard God's reassurance so clearly: "Christy, you can trust again. This person will take care of your needs."

I don't believe God broke my ankle to teach me a lesson, but I do believe He used that challenging experience to show me what I needed to see. Sometimes our greatest fears—in my case, whether I would ever have someone truly care for my needs—are answered in unexpected ways. That broken ankle became the foundation for a healed heart.

The man carrying my laundry basket was showing me who he truly was. Not through words or promises, but through consistent, loving actions when I was at my most vulnerable. And if I could trust him with my physical care when I couldn't do for myself, perhaps I could also trust him with my heart when it was equally fragile.

Blending families has been both our greatest challenge and our greatest opportunity for growth. Between us, we have five children—my two daughters and his three sons with a 15-year age gap. Each child brings their own history, their own wounds, their own ways of trusting or not trusting.

What makes it work is our commitment to honest communication—not just between us, but with all the children. We've created a space where feelings can be expressed without judgment, where differences can be acknowledged without creating division.

When my daughters struggle with any relationship or issue, Beau is careful not to overstep. "I'm not trying to replace your father," he tells her. "This is just another perspective." His own sons have taught me about patience, about how love can grow naturally when it's not forced, that I needed their love in my life. They are so complimentary of me, and Beau encourages that. He tells me the things he wants his sons to learn from me and shares my strengths with them. I had no idea that I needed this kind of relationship from these children.

I've seen the impact of his parenting style firsthand. One day, his middle son fell off his bike and afterward was afraid to ride again. I shared with him the story from my childhood —how when my sister and I were thrown from a horse, my father made us get back on and ride all the way back to the barn. At the time, I was furious, but it taught me resilience.

Beau took a gentler approach with his son, encouraging without forcing, and eventually, the boy got back on his bike. The pride in his face when he conquered that fear showcased that there are many ways to teach important life lessons. Sometimes the gentle path can be just as effective as the tough one. And together, in our newly created family, we'll find the methods that work the best for us.

The practical aspects of blending families have taught us creativity in trust-building. We've learned to navigate holidays, schedules, and blend our similar parenting styles. When Beau's sons stay with us, we create space for their routines while gently introducing new ones. When my daughters need time just with me, we honor their pace. It's a delicate dance of respecting what was while building what will be.

One of the most beautiful aspects of this new chapter is watching our children learn from our example. They see what healthy partnership looks like in both big moments and everyday routines. They observe us helping each other with daily tasks that are very visible to them—prepping dinner together, doing dishes side by side, sharing responsibilities that don't fall on just one person. They witness how two people can have different perspectives without one having to be wrong. They observe how trust can be rebuilt, how love can be both fierce and gentle. These seemingly small moments of cooperation are actually powerful lessons about respect, teamwork, and what genuine partnership looks like.

THE PERMISSION TO BEGIN AGAIN

New beginnings are an act of faith. Not faith that everything will be perfect, but faith in yourself—your strength, your wisdom, your ability to handle whatever comes. It's trusting that your past has prepared you, not defined you.

Starting over is a chance to reclaim your narrative. You get to decide what this next chapter looks like—not just in relationships, but in every area of your life. You get to redefine what trust, love, and partnership mean to you. You get to decide who you want to be in this new phase of your journey.

Is it scary? Absolutely. New beginnings always require a leap of faith. But perhaps that's what makes them so profound. Because in the end, the most life-changing leaps aren't just about jumping into something new. They're about jumping into a new version of yourself—the version that knows she can face the unknown, because she trusts the strength within herself.

As you contemplate your own new beginning, consider:

- What is one small way you can practice honoring your intuition today?

- Reflect on the people in your life. Who

encourages you to trust yourself? Who makes
you doubt yourself?

- What old stories about yourself are you ready to
release? What new stories are you ready to
embrace?

You're not starting from zero. You're starting from all the
wisdom, resilience, and self-awareness you've gained along
the way. You're starting from a place of deepened understanding—of yourself, your needs, and what you deserve.

As you step forward, let your intuition guide you. Let
your boundaries protect you. And let your courage inspire
you. Because here's the truth: You've already survived so
much. You've already proven your strength in a thousand
quiet ways. You've already shown that you can rise from the
ashes, time and again.

Trust that you have what it takes. Trust that your story
isn't over—it's just turning to a new chapter, one that you
get to write for yourself.

PART FOUR
LIVING IN TRUST

CHAPTER TWELVE

TRUSTING YOUR BRAIN AND BODY

OUR LIMITATIONS AREN'T REALLY ABOUT THE CIRCUMSTANCES WE face—they're about the stories we tell ourselves about those circumstances. The narrative we create becomes the cage that either constrains us or the foundation that propels us forward.

For many years, I told myself a story about not being enough. Not thin enough, not accomplished enough, not a good enough mother. These stories became the invisible boundaries of my life, the lines I was afraid to cross.

Sometimes our deepest limitations come from those moments when we've lost faith in ourselves. A life coach of mine used to say, "Stay curious." I nodded along when she said it, but I didn't really get it—not in my bones—until I went through the experience of completely losing trust in myself after the triple storm I experienced.

There I was, someone who prided herself on making good decisions, on knowing the right path forward, suddenly questioning everything. How could I trust my judgment about anything when I'd been so wrong about something so fundamental? Each morning I'd wake up with that knot of doubt in my stomach, that voice whispering, "Who are you to make this decision when you messed up the last one so badly?"

As I began to rebuild myself, I made a subtle but powerful shift. I decided that even if I couldn't trust myself, I could trust God. And so I became curious—genuinely, openly curious—about where He was guiding me. I'd wake up and instead of that knot of self-doubt, I'd feel a gentle wondering: "What are you showing me today? Where are we going?"

What happened next surprised me. Through this practice of staying curious about God's guidance, I gradually learned to trust His voice within me, distinguishing between the noise of fear and the quiet certainty of guidance.

Unlike external obstacles that we can see and strategize around, inner limitations operate below the surface. They're the silent saboteurs that whisper "you can't" when opportunity knocks, "you don't deserve this" when success appears, "this isn't meant for someone like you" when dreams beckon.

But every limitation has a gift hidden within it. Every wound carries the seed of strength. Every struggle contains the blueprint for resilience.

I remember being in therapy, trying to figure out why I kept having these triggering emotional reactions to Beau's facial expressions. The way his eyebrows raise and his forehead crinkles in certain moments would send me spiraling unexpectedly. He's naturally expressive—he was a theater major, after all—and sometimes I'd catch a look on his face that would trigger an immediate defensive response in me.

During one particularly powerful session, my therapist leaned forward and asked something so simple: "You were trained at a very young age to read body language, weren't you?"

And just like that, everything clicked.

Growing up with my dad, I learned to read the room the second he walked in. The way he placed his keys on the counter, the tone of his first words—these tiny signals told me what kind of evening we'd have. He was a brilliant physician who carried the weight of life-and-death decisions daily, and that intensity naturally extended into our home life. His high standards and expectations weren't born from harshness but from a deep belief in our potential. Still, I became hyper-vigilant, always scanning for the smallest shifts in mood or energy, learning to anticipate and adapt to keep things smooth.

What I didn't realize was how deeply that wiring had embedded itself in my brain. Decades later, Beau would make a perfectly innocent expression—maybe just thinking about something practical—and my brain would immediately go into protection mode. All of a sudden, I'd be unregulated, defensive, ready for a fight that wasn't even happening.

"When you read his reactions," my therapist explained, "your brain is immediately trained from childhood to go, 'Oh, this equals this.' But that's not the truth with each person."

The wiring that protects us in one season can limit us in another. What once kept you safe may now be keeping you small. But the beautiful truth is this: we can rewire these patterns. God designed our brains with incredible neuroplasticity—the ability to transform how we respond to the world around us.

Our brains develop these protective patterns for good reasons. That hypervigilance kept me safe as a child. That people-pleasing, being voted "Most Friendly" in high school, wasn't just about being nice; it helped me navigate unpredictable environments. I was making myself digestible. Likable. Someone people could trust to be kind. I was being who people needed me to be because I wanted to be the girl who was invited in.

The journey of rewiring begins with recognition. I had to first see these patterns for what they were—adaptive responses that had outlived their usefulness. My tendency to spiral when Beau made certain expressions wasn't me being "dramatic"; it was my brain's way of trying to protect me from being blindsided again.

In another breakthrough therapy session, my therapist asked me to close my eyes and notice what happened in my body when I felt triggered. "Where do you feel it first?" she asked. I realized it started as a tightening in my chest, then moved to my shoulders, which would hunch up toward my ears. My jaw would clench without my even noticing.

"That's your nervous system activating," she explained. "It's not logical—it's physiological. Your body is reacting before your conscious mind has time to assess the real situation."

What I had interpreted as a personal failing was actually my brain's protective mechanism—one that had served me well as a child but was now misreading the signals in my adult relationships.

Once I recognized these patterns, I could begin the gentle work of creating new ones.

When Beau made a face that triggered me, I learned to pause and ask: "Is this about now, or is this about then?" I'd literally have to say to myself, "This is Beau, not my ex-husband." Sometimes I'd need to take a moment to regulate my breathing, to remind my body that I was safe.

This rewiring work isn't only about relationships. I see it in how I abandoned some of my deepest passions because I was afraid of how others would perceive me. I loved fashion. I dreamed about that world of modeling and design. But I buried that passion so deep that even now, decades later, I struggle to own it. I worried that embracing it would make people think I was conceited, that I thought I was "all that." Looking back, I can see how I learned to doubt my own dreams, to choose security over what truly lit me up inside. And that pattern has repeated itself in so many areas of my life.

During EMDR therapy in my forties, I uncovered how deeply I'd been affected by certain experiences in my youth. Through this specialized therapy, I was able to process traumatic memories that I had buried for decades.

One particular EMDR session stands out. As we worked through a painful memory, my therapist guided me to notice my physical sensations. "What are you feeling in your body right now?" she asked. I felt a heaviness in my chest, almost like I couldn't breathe fully.

"That sensation is carrying information," she explained. "It's holding the emotions you weren't allowed to express back then."

As we processed that memory, something extraordinary happened. The heaviness began to lift, replaced by a feeling of expansion I hadn't experienced before. It was as if a weight I'd been carrying for decades was finally being set down.

I'd carried that wiring for years without even knowing it was there. These moments of silent programming happen to all of us. Maybe it was being told you were too sensitive, too dramatic, too much or not enough. Maybe it was having your feelings dismissed, your dreams redirected, your instincts questioned.

For years, scientists believed that once our brains developed in childhood, they were relatively fixed. We now know that's not true. Our brains can adapt, change, and create new connections well into adulthood.

This science can give us hope. It means that no matter how deeply ingrained our patterns are, change is possible. Not overnight, but gradually, with patience and practice.

SELF-REGULATION: THE KEY TO REWIRING

Growing up, emotions weren't something we indulged in—they were slightly an inconvenience. My father as a physician and a farmer dealt with serious things all the time. His language was action, not words. That was not a fault, but more so his training. And the unspoken lesson in our house was clear: emotions were not something you spent time on. You pushed forward, ignored them, and carried on. It wasn't a harsh message; it was just to keep us focused on moving forward.

I carried that same mentality into adulthood, straight into my marriage. In both cases of my childhood and marriage, I learned that expressing my emotions led to dismissal, often met with those dreaded words: that I'm creating issues. I hated that. I learned to dismiss my emotions because they were considered wrong. I did not learn to communicate effectively through them until Beau. For most of my life, I internalized the message that my feelings were invalid, exaggerated, or problematic—which left me questioning my own intuition and reality.

I became a master of distraction—which gave me tremendous success in business. But the body keeps score. And when my marriage ended, my nervous system betrayed me. Panic attacks. Shaking hands. Racing thoughts. My cortisol levels were insanely high having lived in fight or flight for so many years. My body would physically ache. My head couldn't remember things, and I was just going through the motions. It was as if every suppressed feeling had come back with interest, demanding to be dealt with.

If you're wondering where to start with your own rewiring, here's a structured approach that has helped me and many others:

1. Identify Your Triggers and Patterns
Start by becoming aware of when you feel emotionally dysregulated or find yourself falling into behaviors that don't serve you. Ask yourself:

- What situations consistently trigger strong emotional responses?
- What are the physical sensations that accompany these triggers?
- What are your automatic thoughts or beliefs in these moments?
- How do you typically respond (shut down, lash out, people-please, etc.)?

Keep a journal for a week and note each time you feel triggered. Look for patterns in situations, people, or even times
of day.

2. Trace the Origins

For each pattern you identify, explore its origins:

- When did I first learn this response?
- What was happening in my life at that time?
- How did this pattern serve me then?
- Who modeled this behavior for me?

Understanding the origins helps you approach yourself with
compassion rather than judgment. These patterns developed for a reason—they were your mind's best attempt to
keep you safe.

3. Create a Pause

The key to changing automatic responses is creating space
between trigger and reaction. Practice pausing when you
notice yourself getting triggered:

- Take three deep breaths
- Name what you're feeling: "I'm feeling anxious
  right now"
- Ask yourself: "Is this about now, or about then?"

This pause interrupts the automatic circuit and gives your
rational brain time to catch up with your emotional
response.

4. Develop New Responses

Once you've created that pause, you can begin practicing new responses:

- If you tend to people-please, practice saying, "Let me think about that and get back to you"
- If you catastrophize, try asking, "What's the most likely outcome here?"
- If you withdraw when hurt, experiment with stating your feelings directly

Start with low-stakes situations to build confidence before tackling more challenging ones.

Learning to regulate myself has been a journey of small steps and consistent practice. Here are some of the techniques that have helped me move from emotional overwhelm to emotional freedom:

Mindful Breathing
I've learned that we can change our emotional state by changing our breathing. When I feel that familiar tightness in my chest, I take slow, deliberate breaths. Inhaling for 4 counts, holding for 7, and exhaling for 8. Sometimes I'll place my hand on my heart or my stomach to feel the rise and fall, reminding myself that I'm here, I'm safe, and this feeling will pass.

Creating Distance from Thoughts
One of the most powerful tools I've learned is that thoughts are not facts. When my mind starts racing with catastrophic thinking, I practice saying, "I notice I'm having the thought that..." This small linguistic shift

creates space between me and the thought, allowing me to see it as just that—a thought, not reality. I've also named the thoughts "Irene" so I can separate myself from her when needed.

Movement as Regulation
Sometimes emotions are too big to think our way through. That's when I turn to movement. A walk around the block. Stretching my arms overhead. Even just shaking out my hands and feet. Physical movement helps release the energy that gets trapped in our bodies during emotional distress.

Loving-Kindness Meditation
When self-criticism takes over, I practice directing kindness toward myself with phrases like:
• May I be safe
• May I be healthy
• May I be at peace
• May I live with ease
This practice reminds me that I deserve the same compassion I so readily offer others.

I've also learned that self-regulation isn't about doing it alone. I used to believe that strength meant handling everything myself, but I now know that healing happens in community. Whether it's through therapy, close friends, or prayer, allowing myself to be supported has been one of the most powerful shifts in my life.

Prayer grounds me in something greater than my immediate emotions. When anxiety builds, I turn to scripture, repeating truths that remind me I am not alone. Isaiah 41:10 became my anchor: "Do not fear, for I am with you; do not be dismayed, for I am your God. I will strengthen you and help you; I will uphold you with my righteous right hand."

SEEING RESULTS IN REAL LIFE

One thing I've learned in my rewiring journey is the importance of celebrating progress, no matter how small it seems. Recently, I had a situation with Beau where I noticed my chest tightening in response to another expression on his face. In the past, I would have immediately jumped to defensiveness or withdrawal.

This time, I took a breath and said to myself, "This is not what I think. This reaction isn't about the present—it's about the past. I need a moment to center myself."

That small moment—choosing awareness and communication over reaction—represented years of work. And Beau's response—giving me space without taking my reaction personally—showed me how healing happens not just individually but in relationship.

These small wins might not seem significant to others, but they're the building blocks of transformation. Each time we respond differently, we're strengthening new neural pathways and weakening the old ones.

The other day, Kate came home frustrated after a difficult day at school. Instead of immediately trying to fix it or telling her it wasn't a big deal, I simply sat beside her and said, "That sounds really hard. I'm here with you." She leaned her head on my shoulder, and I could feel the tension begin to release. In that moment, I realized I was giving her what I had always needed—permission to feel without judgment.

Learning to identify when I'm becoming dysregulated

has also transformed my relationships. I now recognize the early warning signs—that slight irritation that feels disproportionate, the defensiveness that rises quickly, the urge to withdraw or lash out.

When Beau and I disagree, I've learned to say, "I need a moment to regulate myself before we continue this conversation." It's my responsibility. It's recognizing that I can't show up as my best self when my nervous system is in fight, flight, or freeze mode.

The space between stimulus and response is where our power lies. And the more I practice creating that space through self-regulation, the more I can choose how I want to respond rather than being driven by automatic reactions.

You're not trying to become someone new. You're uncovering who you've been all along beneath the layers of protection and adaptation. The real you—the one God created—has always been there, waiting to be rediscovered.

I love what Romans 12:2 says about being "transformed by the renewing of your mind." That's exactly what rewiring is—a process that's both spiritual and neurological.

In my faith journey, I've come to see this rewiring work as deeply spiritual. God designed our brains with this incredible capacity for change. When I'm doing the hard work of creating new patterns, I'm cooperating with divine design.

I've found prayer to be powerful in this journey—not just asking God to change me, but inviting Him to show me how He sees me, to help me understand His truth about who I am. When old tapes play in my head—"You're too much," "You're not enough"—I counter them with truths about how God sees me.

The old wiring doesn't have to determine your future.

Those early experiences shaped you, but they don't have to define you. The patterns feel automatic now, but they don't have to stay that way.

You can learn to trust yourself again—not by dismissing your past, but by integrating it with compassion; not by ignoring your triggers, but by understanding them; not by pretending old wounds don't exist, but by allowing them to heal.

The truth is, that inner knowing—the same wisdom that helped a seventh-grade girl visualize her way back to strength after an injury, the same intuition that told me something was wrong in my marriage long before I had proof—never really leaves us. It just gets buried under years of learning to doubt ourselves.

Take some time to consider these questions as you begin your own rewiring journey:

• What early experiences shaped how you handle challenges today? Think about times when you were taught to doubt yourself or push down your feelings.

• When were you taught that your instincts or emotions weren't trustworthy? How does that still show up in your life?

• Think of a time when you knew something deep down but talked yourself out of it. What might have been different if you'd trusted that knowing?

• Which relationships in your life make it easier for you to trust yourself? Which makes it harder?

• What would be possible in your life if you could fully trust your ability to rewire old patterns?

• What small step could you take today to begin creating new patterns?

God doesn't waste any of our experiences. Not the triumphs, not the falls, not even those moments when we realize we've been operating from old wiring that no longer serves us. It's all preparation for something bigger than we can see at the time.

And that's the greatest hope in all of this: the truest version of yourself hasn't been lost. It's just been waiting for you to create the conditions where it can finally, fully emerge.

CHAPTER THIRTEEN

TRUSTING EACH STEP FORWARD

"You lean in and let Him guide you. Things unfold in His time, not yours. He knows better than you. His way is easier than yours."

I wrote these words in my journal late one night, trying to make sense of the doors that kept opening in unexpected directions. Life had taught me that sometimes the best paths forward aren't the ones we carefully plan, but the ones that reveal themselves when we're brave enough to take that first step.

My daughter Christine wasn't specifically hunting down a particular internship. She was just taking small steps, having conversations with different people, exploring possibilities. She'd been in touch with one company for months. They didn't have anything available at first, but someone she spoke with mentioned they knew about another opportunity that could be a good fit for her.

What's crazy is how perfectly all the pieces aligned in a way only God could orchestrate. As you now know, Christine is legitimately goth—I mean, you should see her room sometime! It's the complete opposite of the little girl who couldn't even handle Halloween decorations. Back then, we couldn't have a skeleton or a clown—everything had to be jack-o'-lanterns and mermaids. Now she loves being in cemeteries. It used to seem very strange to me, but it's genuinely who she is and it has helped her overcome her fear with death.

She also absolutely loves plants. She was a plant and soil science major at Texas Tech for two years, and her knowledge of indoor plants is insane for a 22-year-old. Her ability to care for them is just remarkable. Then she transferred schools and switched to geography and sustainability.

So, this internship opportunity shows up, and it's literally working with a nonprofit that helps revitalize five underserved cemeteries in Dallas. And Christine would be helping with the choices of plants! I mean, seriously—what are the chances? She didn't go seeking a plant internship in cemeteries. This just appeared, combining everything she loves.

When she got the news, her face lit up in a way I hadn't seen in months. This is a girl who's struggled with believing in herself, who was very bright but had trouble applying herself. So seeing her feel this pride, this sense of "Oh my gosh, mom, they want me"—it was everything.

And this wasn't the only door opening. The same week, this store where she lives reached out about interviewing her for a job. She'd won two giveaways from their Instagram and they already knew her. Then she started going to Pilates and called me afterward saying, "It was amazing; it was the most peaceful environment."

"Christine, look," I told her as all these things were happening at once. "This is God showing up for you. Even with everything weighing you down right now, He's showing you that He's got you. This is your life. He's guiding you and telling you through these opening doors to keep going forward."

That's what I want her to learn—to be cognizant of these signs, to practice seeing them. When the doors open, it's like He's saying "I've got you, this is your life. Stay the course, don't get caught back in all the fears. Your future is ahead, not behind."

When we trust this, we're not saying that nothing bad will happen. We're saying that whatever happens, we'll find a way through it. It's knowing that while we can't control everything that happens to us, we can trust our ability to respond with courage and creativity.

Watching Christine navigate these opening doors reminded me so much of my own journey—how I've had to learn to trust each step even when I couldn't see the entire path. The way doors opened unexpectedly for her mirrored how God has worked in my own life, particularly during the hardest seasons when my carefully constructed plans fell apart.

For most of my life, I approached major decisions with what I now call "blueprint thinking." I wanted the entire path mapped out before I took the first step. I wanted guarantees, certainties, clear outcomes. I wanted God to show me the whole staircase, not just the next step.

This approach made sense given my upbringing. My father was a meticulous planner who believed in having clear goals and direct paths to achieve them. In our family, spontaneity was not in our vocabulary, and "going with the flow" was practically a character flaw. Success came through careful planning and methodical execution.

But life has a way of dismantling our illusions of control, doesn't it?

Cancer didn't fit into my carefully constructed life plan. Neither did divorce. Or being sued by a company I had helped build. None of these experiences were part of my blueprint.

In the aftermath of these disruptions, I had to learn a completely different approach to navigating life—what I now think of as watching for signs or little nudges. Instead of demanding to see the entire path illuminated at once, I learned to stay curious for the next small indicator of where to go.

I've come to see that there are two ways to approach life's journey:

The Blueprint Approach: This is where you try to map out everything in advance. You want guarantees, certainties, and clear outcomes before taking action. While planning has its place, this approach often leaves us paralyzed when life doesn't follow our script.

The Breadcrumb Approach: This is where you stay open to divine guidance, taking each step as it's revealed, trusting that the next will become clear when you need it. This approach requires faith, flexibility, and comfort with uncertainty, but it often leads to places more wonderful than we could have planned.

A sign to move forward might be a random conversation that sparks an idea. It might be an unexpected opportunity that aligns with your gifts. It might be a door that opens when all others have closed.

This approach requires something the blueprint approach doesn't: trust. You have to trust that the next sign will appear when you need it. You have to trust that you'll recognize it when it does. You have to trust that each step is leading somewhere meaningful, even when you can't see the destination.

AN INNER ARCHAEOLOGICAL DIG

But how do you know which steps to take when you're not even sure what you want or need anymore? How do you hear that still, small voice inside when it's been drowned out by everyone else's perspectives for so long?

That's the question I wrestled with after my divorce. When your identity has been wrapped up in a relationship or a role for decades, it can be terrifying to figure out who you really are without those labels. The decisions we make are linked to who we believe we are. You have to learn how to trust yourself to make decisions again.

For me, rediscovering my own values and boundaries was like archaeological work—digging through layers of approval seeking and compromise to find what was truly mine. I realized I'd spent years compromising and not following my own compass and values. It's not that I didn't have values of my own; it's that I'd buried them under everyone else's needs.

I remember sitting in my rental house after leaving our marital home, surrounded by boxes, wondering: What do I actually care about? What matters to ME as a grown woman? Not what should matter, not what that little girl thought should matter to her parents, not what would look good to other people—but what resonated in my soul.

Financial security? Yes, but not at the expense of emotional health. I'd watched my grandmother save ketchup packets from restaurants to stretch every penny. That frugality was ingrained in me. But I was learning that sometimes spending money on therapy or a rental house that gave me peace was the wisest investment I could make.

Family connection? Absolutely, but with healthy boundaries. I felt this inner yearning to learn to rely on myself for the first time. I had not trusted myself. The Cuban side of my family and their story had taught me that family sticks together no matter what—a beautiful value that had also sometimes had me making decisions based on what family might expect versus what my heart wanted. I was learning that love and boundaries could coexist.

Faith? Deeper than ever, but practiced in a way that felt authentic to me, not someone else's interpretation. I'd grown up thinking faith was just structure and rules; now I was discovering it as a relationship of trust.

Setting boundaries was even harder. I'd grown up believing that putting others first was the ultimate virtue. I began at a young age wanting others to be proud of me. So much so that I would make decisions based on that. But I was learning that boundaries aren't selfish—they're necessary. Without them, I had nothing genuine to offer this world. I wasn't truly using the strengths and gifts that I was given to make a difference. I had an obligation to myself and my purpose in this world to be my true authentic self.

This became even more challenging when I started dating again. I was so eager because I was starved for a healthy connection and attention. But I had to be careful not to get swept away by that hunger.

I wasn't looking for someone to "complete" me—I was

looking for someone who would respect the boundaries and values I was finally brave enough to claim. I wanted true partnership and fun. Someone who would bring out the best in me, and me in him.

That's why I didn't immediately share with many close to me who I was dating. What I was attracted to or needed now wasn't necessarily what they would possibly choose for me. I had to learn to find me, and that meant sometimes creating space to hear my own voice without the well-meaning input of others who loved me.

One of my best friends went through something similar recently. After getting out of a difficult relationship, she started dating someone new and was terrified to tell her friends. "They'll try to protect me," she said. "They'll have opinions. But I need to feel this out for myself first."

It's not that those who loved us were wrong—they just weren't us. They hadn't lived inside our marriages; they hadn't felt what we'd felt; they hadn't craved what we did not have. What was best for me wouldn't be what was best for everyone else. Learning to distinguish this was hard for me, but necessary.

DISCERNING DIVINE DIRECTION

One of the most significant shifts in my spiritual life has been learning to recognize God's guidance through those open and closed doors rather than just through feelings or circumstances.

In the past, I often mistook emotional responses for divine direction. If something felt good, I assumed it was God's will. If something felt hard, I questioned whether I was on the right path. But emotions can be unreliable guides, influenced by everything from lack of sleep to past trauma to what we ate for breakfast.

I've learned to look for something more concrete, such as those doors that open or close despite logical expectations.

Like when Beau's landlady held a rental property for him without a deposit or contract—something that made no financial sense in the competitive Dallas rental market. Or when Kate received a substantial scholarship to her dream school in New York without even applying for it. Or when Christine found an internship that perfectly combined her love of plants with her fascination with cemeteries—a combination so specific it couldn't have been coincidence.

These open doors were divine breadcrumbs guiding us toward paths that aligned with our authentic selves and God's purposes for our lives.

But discerning which doors to walk through isn't always straightforward. Sometimes multiple doors stand open, and we have to choose. Other times, no doors seem to be opening at all, and we feel stuck in a hallway of waiting.

Over time, I've developed a framework for discerning which doors to walk through:

1. The Peace Test

As we discussed in Chapter 9, our inner peace can be a powerful truth-teller. When considering a potential path, I pay attention to whether it brings deep peace or unsettling anxiety. Not the temporary anxiety that comes with any significant change, but a persistent sense of misalignment.

When Kate was considering colleges, she had several good options. But when she talked about the school in New

York, there was a lightness in her voice, a clarity in her eyes that wasn't there when she discussed other schools. Her entire being seemed at peace with that direction, despite the practical challenges it presented.

It was both far and expensive. But I saw how her face lit up when she talked about it. I saw how this school had offered her a $128,000 scholarship over four years without us even applying for one. I saw doors opening.

2. The Confirmation Pattern

Divine direction often comes through multiple confirmations rather than a single sign. When several unrelated sources point toward the same path, it's worth paying attention.

When I was considering leaving pharmaceutical sales for a direct sales opportunity, I initially dismissed it as too risky. But then several trusted mentors independently suggested I consider it. A friend sent me an article about women finding flexibility and purpose in similar roles. My sister, who had built a business of her own, encouraged me to try it. My devotional reading that week focused on stepping out in faith. These weren't dramatic signs, but together they created a pattern I couldn't ignore.

3. The Counsel of Community

While we shouldn't base our decisions solely on others' opinions, there's wisdom in seeking counsel from people who know us well and have our best interests at heart.

When Beau and I were dating and considering whether he should move across the street from me, we didn't make that decision in isolation. We sought wisdom from our closest friends, my therapist, and spiritual mentors. Their insights helped us see potential challenges we hadn't considered and affirmed the strengths they saw in our relationship.

4. The Alignment Check

Any direction from God will align with His character as revealed in Scripture. It won't contradict His nature or His commands.

This doesn't mean the path will be easy or safe by worldly standards. Jesus never promised His followers comfort or convenience. But it does mean the direction won't require you to compromise your integrity or violate core biblical principles.

5. The Persistent Return

Sometimes a particular direction keeps presenting itself even after you've dismissed it. Like a boomerang that keeps coming back, it refuses to be ignored.

For years, I felt a nudge to write this book, but I made excuses: I wasn't a writer, my story wasn't finished, who would want to read it anyway? But the prompting persisted through different seasons and circumstances. Friends would randomly suggest I should write a book. Strangers would respond to my social media posts saying my words should be in a book. Eventually, I had to pay attention to this persistent pattern. My business coach told me that this burning desire would not go away until I did something about it. He was right.

. . .

One of the most powerful tools I found for getting clear on my values and boundaries was simply asking myself: "What feels right to me?"

This question helped me navigate everything from career decisions to parenting challenges to relationships. When I was torn about whether to let Kate go to college in New York—which felt scary and expensive—or have her "play it safe" at a local school like her sister, I kept coming back to: What feels right for her? Not what's easiest for me, not what looks best on paper, but what aligns with who she is and what she needs.

I've learned that divine guidance often works when we take that first step in faith. It's like my Bible study leader says: "God can't steer a parked car." You have to be moving, even if it's just small steps, to see which way the path is leading.

Sometimes, despite our best efforts at discernment, the next step simply isn't clear. Doors haven't opened, breadcrumbs haven't appeared, and we find ourselves in what feels like a hallway of waiting.

These waiting seasons can be agonizing, especially for action-oriented people like me. My father's voice echoes in my head: "Idle hands are the devil's workshop." I want to be productive, to make progress, to see tangible results. Waiting feels like wasting time.

But I've learned that waiting isn't passive when it's done with purpose. Holy waiting is active, expectant, and surprisingly productive in ways that aren't always visible.

Anytime I felt stuck between my old life and whatever was coming next, I discovered practices that transformed my waiting from empty frustration to meaningful preparation:

1. Presence Practice

Instead of constantly straining to see what was next, I learned to be fully present where I was. I practiced mindfulness—really tasting my food, really listening when my daughters spoke, really noticing the beauty around me. I started spending time with girlfriends more spontaneously because suddenly I had the time. This wasn't about denying my desire for clarity; it was about recognizing that life was happening now, not just in some future when everything became clear.

2. Preparation Without Specifics

I couldn't prepare for what I didn't know was coming, but I could develop skills and qualities that would serve me well regardless of what lay ahead. I could strengthen my resilience, deepen my faith, improve my health, nurture my relationships. These investments would bear fruit no matter what door eventually opened.

3. Walking in Trust

Sometimes we need to take action even without complete clarity, not as a final commitment but as a way of gathering more information. This is about moving forward in trust—taking small steps that can be adjusted as more becomes clear.

· · ·

4. Journaling

One of my most meaningful waiting practices became journaling. I would pour my questions, hopes, fears, and observations onto paper, creating a dialogue between my conscious thoughts and deeper knowing. Something about this written exploration created space for insights to emerge. I wasn't just waiting; I was actively seeking, listening, processing.

During these journaling sessions, I would often receive what felt like downloads of wisdom—not necessarily specific answers to my questions, but shifts in perspective that helped me see my situation differently.

Looking back now, I can see how each small step—each time I trusted my own voice even when it was scary—was preparing me for the life I have now. It didn't happen because I had the whole journey mapped out. It happened because I kept taking the next step that opened before me, even when I couldn't see where it would lead. Honestly, I would not change a thing, but it has taken a long while to feel that way.

Take a moment to consider:

• What small step is opening up before you that you've been hesitating to take?

• Where in your life are you waiting for the whole path to be clear before moving forward?

• How might your journey change if you trusted the

step in front of you instead of needing to see the whole staircase?

The truth is, we often want God to give us the whole blueprint when He's really just asking us to take the next step. We want certainty when He's offering guidance. We want a map when He's offering a compass.

Trusting each step doesn't mean you never feel fear—it means you don't let fear have the final say. It doesn't mean you always know where the path is leading—it means you trust that each step is preparing you for what's ahead.

Sometimes the most important steps don't look important at all when we're taking them. That first "yes" to a jewelry party didn't look like a career change. That first conversation with Beau didn't look like the beginning of a beautiful blended family. That first step rarely looks like the journey it will become.

But the path becomes clear in time. Because sometimes the very step you're afraid to take is the one that leads exactly where you need to go.

What step is opening before you today?

CHAPTER FOURTEEN

TRUSTING YOURSELF AND THE WHOLE JOURNEY

As our journey together comes to a close, I want to circle back to where we began, but with new eyes. You're not the same person who started reading these pages. You've walked through stories of brokenness and healing, of lost trust and rediscovered strength. Now it's time to gather what we've learned and carry it forward into your own unfolding story.

Throughout this book, we've explored four pillars that form the bedrock of a life anchored in self-trust. These aren't just concepts to understand—they're practices to embody, day by day, choice by choice:

Trusting Your Perception—This first pillar means honoring what you see, feel, and experience without requiring external validation. It's standing in your truth even when others can't or won't see it. It's saying, "This is what I'm experiencing," and knowing that's enough. When you trust your perception, you move through the world with clarity that isn't dependent on others' approval or under-standing.

Trusting Your Resilience—This pillar means believing in your capacity to handle whatever outcomes arise—even the painful ones. It's not about avoiding failure or heartbreak; it's about knowing that whatever comes, you'll find your way through. When you trust your resilience, you can take risks, love boldly, and live fully because you know that whatever happens, you'll handle it.

Trusting Your Decisions—Here's where rubber meets road: developing the confidence to make choices aligned with your authentic self, even when they disappoint people you love. It's having the courage to say, "This is right for me," and truly believing it. When you trust your decisions, you escape the prison of people-pleasing and step into the freedom of authoring your own life.

Trusting Your Wisdom—This pillar acknowledges that your life experiences—especially the difficult ones—have given you insights that deserve profound respect, particu-larly from yourself. Your hard-earned wisdom isn't just valuable; it's essential. The lessons you've gathered through tears and triumph have shaped you into someone with a unique perspective that the world desperately needs.

When these pillars are strong, you walk through life with a quiet confidence that doesn't depend on perfect circumstances. Storms may come—they will come—but you'll stand firm because you're anchored in something unshakable: trust in the person God created you to be.

Faith isn't just a part of my story—it's the foundation beneath every word I've written. God doesn't call us to be watered-down versions of ourselves. He calls us to live fully, boldly, authentically as the people He created us to be.

When I think about authenticity, I think about Jesus. He didn't spend His life conforming to others' expectations. He didn't shrink to make people comfortable. He spoke truth. He lived truth. Even when it cost Him everything.

And if we are made in His image, why would we be called to anything less?

During my darkest days, when I was questioning everything I thought I knew about myself, I remember crying out, "God, who am I, really? Who am I beneath all these roles and expectations?" The answer didn't come in a thunderbolt revelation. It came in gentle nudges—books that seemed to find me at just the right moment, verses that suddenly took on new meaning, the inexplicable peace that would settle over me when I finally made decisions that honored my deepest knowing.

I started paying attention to those breadcrumbs of divine guidance. The doors that opened when I stepped into greater authenticity. The sense of alignment I felt when I honored the voice God had placed within me. And a beautiful pattern emerged: the more I trusted the person God created me to be, the more my external life began to reflect that inner knowing.

This isn't prosperity gospel—living authentically won't shield you from hardship. In fact, it will cost you something. It might cost you relationships built on a false version of yourself. It will certainly cost you the comfort of playing it safe. It will cost you the approval of people who benefited from your smaller self.

But what will you gain?

Peace that surpasses understanding. Energy that comes from living in alignment. Freedom from the exhaustion of pretending. And most profoundly—a life that actually feels like yours.

When you finally stop trying to be who the world wants you to be, you become available to be who God created you to be. And that kind of alignment? It's both satisfying *and* sacred.

The Invitation: Your Turn to Trust Again

I want to offer you something as we part ways: transformation. An invitation to trust yourself again. Not because you have all the answers, but because you have something even more valuable: your own unique wisdom, shaped by every experience you've lived through.

Those storms that were meant to break you? They revealed your strength instead. Those moments of confusion that were meant to silence you? They prepared you to speak your truth. Those seasons of doubt that were meant to derail you? They ultimately led you home to yourself.

Nothing in your journey has been wasted. Not the pain. Not the uncertainty. Not the times when trust was broken. All of it—every tear, every setback, every moment you thought you couldn't take another step—has been preparation for this moment. The moment you choose to trust yourself again.

This is about recognizing that the voice within you—that knowing, that intuition, that still small voice that has been trying to guide you all along—is worthy of your trust.

I know this because I've lived it. I've felt the paralyzing

doubt that comes after betrayal, after having your reality questioned, after losing faith in your own judgment. And I also know the indescribable freedom that comes from reclaiming that trust, step by tentative step.

So I extend this invitation with both hands: Will you trust yourself again? Will you honor the wisdom of your experiences? Will you give yourself permission to know what you know?

Because guess what? You don't have to earn the right to trust yourself. You only have to reclaim it.

As you close this book and continue your own unfolding story, I want to leave you with practical ways to strengthen your self-trust muscles every day:

Start with radical self-compassion. Forgive yourself for the times you didn't listen to your inner wisdom. Those moments weren't failures—they were necessary lessons preparing you for now. Speak to yourself with the same grace you'd offer your dearest friend.

Build your own evidence list. Just as I did, start documenting the times your intuition was right. Keep this list somewhere visible and add to it regularly. Let it become tangible proof of your inner knowing.

Practice trusting in small, low-stakes moments. Trust your "no" when something feels draining. Trust your "yes" when something lights you up. Trust your "maybe" when you need more information. Each time you honor what feels true for you, that muscle of self-trust grows stronger.

Curate your circle intentionally. Surround yourself with people who celebrate when you stand in your truth—who make room for your authentic voice to emerge. Distance yourself from those who require you to be smaller, less complex, or more palatable to earn their acceptance.

Release the patterns that no longer serve you. Old habits, limiting beliefs, relationships that require your inauthenticity—let them go with gratitude for what they taught you. They were part of your journey, but they don't need to be part of your destination.

Invite God into your discernment process. Ask for wisdom to distinguish between the true voice of your spirit and the voices of fear, people-pleasing, or old conditioning. The more you practice listening for divine guidance, the more clearly you'll recognize it.

Take courageous action. Self-trust isn't just about inner knowing; it's about outer doing. When you feel that nudge, that knowing, honor it with action—even when it's scary, even when the outcome isn't guaranteed.

For too long, I shaped myself into who I thought I needed to be to be loved, accepted, and safe. Maybe you've done the same. But I want you to hear this truth deep in your bones: real love doesn't require you to shrink. Real connection isn't built on pretense. And God never called you to live a half-life just to make others comfortable.

What would become possible in your life if you fully trusted that who you are is exactly who you're meant to be?

Because that, right there, is the foundation of true freedom. Not freedom from difficulty, but freedom to be fully, gloriously yourself in the midst of it all.

Trust isn't just something we give to others—it's something we owe to ourselves. And sometimes, the most faithful act we can perform is to finally, fully trust the person God created us to be.

Your journey to trusting yourself again starts right here, right now. And though I can't see the details of your path forward, I can tell you this with absolute certainty: it will be more beautiful, more meaningful, and more authentic than anything you could create while living from someone else's script.

The truth that you are worthy of trust.

The truth that your voice matters.

The truth that your journey, with all its twists and turns, has been leading you home to yourself.

Trust that. Trust you.

And watch as your life unfolds in ways more courageous and true than you ever dared imagine.

ACKNOWLEDGMENTS

To my daughters—you are my heartbeat and my reason for writing this book. I wanted my journey to be documented for you so that one day, when life feels heavy, you can look back and see that your mom walked through her own battles and rose again. Even if no one else ever read a single word, I would have written this for you. You've shown me what unconditional love looks like and given my life deeper purpose. My hope is that when your own challenges come, you'll know deep in your hearts that you, too, can rise up and become even more of who you were meant to be.

To my amazing husband, Beau—you have been my greatest supporter every step of the way. You held my hand when the words wouldn't come, pushed me forward when fear crept in, and celebrated every small win along the journey. You read and re-read each chapter, offering honest feedback and endless encouragement. You believed in this book even when I doubted myself and reminded me who this was for when I questioned sharing my story. I could not have done it without you. You've walked beside me through healing, and I'm forever grateful for your love and partnership.

To Brad Bizjack, my high-performance coach—on our very first call, you saw what I couldn't yet see: that this book was buried deep in my soul and wasn't going anywhere until I brought it to life. Thank you for teaching me that those heart tugs and "impossible" dreams that won't let go are often meant to be—and that fear was the only thing standing in my way. You helped me lean into the hard instead of running from it, reminding me that regret comes from silence, not struggle. Thank you for giving me the confidence to finally bring this passion project to life and for walking beside me as I found the courage to believe I was capable and worthy of this dream.

To my sisters, my lifelong anchors—you are my constant. You've loved me through every success and every struggle, through seasons of healing and growth, even when it wasn't easy. You are my best friends, my life partners, and my business partners. Thank you for listening, for laughing, and for believing in me when I couldn't see the light. I couldn't imagine doing life without you.

To my parents—thank you for giving me the foundation that shaped who I am. The work ethic you instilled in me is one of my greatest gifts. It came from your example—your grit and your perseverance. Those roots gave me the strength to pull myself up when life knocked me down and the independence to not just survive, but to truly thrive.

And to my Park Lane team—the Dreamcatchers—thank you for bringing daily focus to something greater than myself. Your resilience, your stories, and your lives have lifted me more times than you know. Helping you chase your own dreams has given my life a deeper sense of purpose. You remind me every day that healing often begins when we step outside ourselves and pour into others.

To everyone who has walked beside me, cheered me on,

or simply believed in me along the way—thank you. Your love, faith, and encouragement have been the heartbeat behind this book, and I am endlessly grateful.

ABOUT THE AUTHOR

Christy Trujillo is a wife, mother of two daughters, and stepmother to three sons. A small-town Texas native and the daughter of a Cuban immigrant and a country doctor-turned-farmer, Christy was raised with deep roots in hard work, humility, and perseverance—values that continue to guide her both personally and professionally.

A breast cancer survivor who also navigated divorce after a two-decade marriage, Christy has learned firsthand what it means to rebuild, refocus, and rise stronger. Her personal journey fuels her passion for helping women move beyond fear and self-doubt to create lives and businesses rooted in confidence, purpose, and authenticity.

Christy leads one of the top-performing teams in the direct sales industry, ranking within the top fraction of one percent of leaders nationwide—a reflection of her commitment to growth, mentorship, and empowering women to achieve success on their own terms. With nearly two decades of experience coaching and mentoring thousands of women, she has developed a reputation for combining heart-led leadership with proven business strategy to build high-performing, purpose-driven teams.

Known for her grounded faith, resilience, and practical wisdom, Christy continues to inspire women to trust their instincts, embrace courage, and step boldly into their full potential—both in business and in life.

https://www.christytrujillo.com/

instagram.com/christytrujillo_
facebook.com/christyctrujillo
linkedin.com/in/christytrujillo

www.ingramcontent.com/pod-product-compliance
Lightning Source LLC
Chambersburg PA
CBHW051309120626
46547CB00015B/2155